OPUS DEI

OPUS DEI

Leadership and Vision in Today's Catholic Church

VITTORIO MESSORI

Translated from the Italian by Gerald Malsbary

REGNERY PUBLISHING, INC.
Washington, D.C.

Library of Congress Cataloging-in-Publication Data

Messori, Vittorio, 1941–
 [Opus Dei. English]
 Opus Dei : leadership and vision in today's Catholic Church / by
Vittorio Messori : translated from the Italian by Gerald Malsbary.
  p. cm.
 Includes index.
 ISBN 0-89526-450-1 (alk. paper)
 1. Opus Dei (Society) I. Title.
BX819.3.068M4513 1997
267'.182—dc21   97-28110
                                                            CIP

Published in the United States by
Regnery Publishing, Inc.
An Eagle Publishing Company
422 First Street, SE, Suite 300
Washington, DC 20003

Distributed to the trade by
National Book Network
4720-A Boston Way
Lanham, MD 20706

Printed on acid-free paper.
Manufactured in the United States of America

10 9 8 7 6 5 4 3 2 1

Books are available in quantity for promotional or premium use. Write to Director of Special Sales, Regnery Publishing, Inc., 422 First Street, SE, Suite 300, Washington, DC 20003, for information on discounts and terms or call (202) 546-5005.

TABLE OF CONTENTS

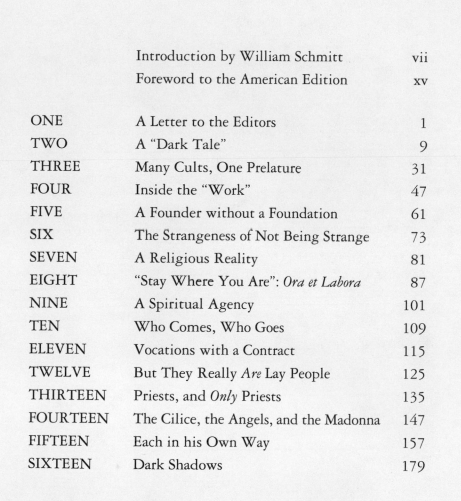

INTRODUCTION

✝

WELL INTO THE THIRD millennium, debate will range far and wide on who had the greatest impact on the world of the twentieth century and beyond. In the fields of science, politics, and literature countless men and women have left lasting contributions, whose effects still are not fully manifest. Less known, but no less significant, will be those who have made a mark on religion and spirituality. Among them will be the name of Josémaría Escrivá, the founder of Opus Dei.

When historians delve into the record of Blessed Josémaría's life and work they will find many surprises, just as Vittorio Messori did in researching this book. Opus Dei's founder, though he did not see himself as such, was nothing short of a revolutionary. He charted a new path in the history of the Church that enables ordinary people—men and women, married and single, young and old—to find God in the midst of their work, family, friends, and social surroundings. Opus Dei, the institution he founded under divine inspiration, is dedicated to spreading this ideal. With the grace of God it has extended across Europe, America, Africa, Asia, and Oceania in the relatively few years since its founding. Its numbers worldwide stand around eighty thousand men and women.

In the United States there are some three thousand members. Since its modest start in Chicago in 1949 it has expanded to about thirty-five cities. Many in this country have benefitted from its apostolic activities. To others it has been a sign of contradiction.

What, more precisely, is the message of Josémaría Escrivá? Namely, that God calls all people to be saints; not just priests, nuns, or men and women religious, but everyone without exception: lawyers, farmers, businessmen and women, professors, students, journalists, among others. Lay people can—indeed must—strive to be saints in and by means of work and ordinary life because this is the only way open to them. Monsignor Escrivá taught an ever old, but ever new, message: that God in his infinite wisdom and goodness has made personal holiness attainable and attractive, and that one should dedicate one's life to the pursuit of personal holiness in whatever activities one is engaged. The quest, in truth, gives new meaning, excitement, and joy—even in the midst of suffering—to all of life. The founder of Opus Dei would agree with Chesterton's assertion that it is not that the faith has been tried and found wanting, but that it has not really been tried.

The spokespersons of Opus Dei, of which I am one, have a penchant for avoiding statistical declarations about the growth of Opus Dei in terms of numbers of buildings, apostolic initiatives, and so on. This comes in part from the founder himself, who insisted that holiness issues from the work of God in souls and cannot be measured in terms of appearances. If there is any glory it belongs to God alone, *Deo omnis gloria*. The lives of the faithful of Opus Dei must speak for themselves. But others, those who are not associated with Opus Dei but who do speak with authority and knowledge, have commented on the life and work of Josémaría Escrivá. They are worth listening to as what they say sheds light not just on the man himself, but on the organization he founded.

Vittorio Messori is not a member of Opus Dei, as he himself states. He is known as an incisive interviewer and writer on Church affairs and is the author of numerous books which have been read by millions. Most recently, his interviews with Pope John Paul II inspired *Crossing the Threshold of Hope*, the Pope's international bestseller. Messori became curious about Opus Dei upon hearing so much about this new phenomenon. He decided to conduct his own investigation and collected data, analyzed it dispassionately, and put it in its proper context. This book, an acclaimed bestseller in Italy, is the result of his enterprise.

Blessed Josémaría Escrivá was a prolific writer. All of his writings, totaling thirteen thousand pages, had been submitted to the Vatican's Congregation for the Causes of the Saints prior to his beatification. The congregation of theological experts judged them thus (as quoted in a 1991 article in the Italian journal *Studi Cattolici*): "Escrivá possesses the strength of the classics: the temper of a Father of the Church." The Vatican congregation continued: "One can see that these writings have preceded and anticipated the most important decisions of Vatican II. They have presented the ideal of ordinary Christian life in direct and fruitful contact with the gospel, which up to now had never appeared in the history of the Church." His writings are a "precious treasure" and "have opened a new era in the Church."

The Catholic faith teaches that souls in Heaven can intercede before Jesus Christ on behalf of those on earth. It is a consoling belief that those who lived a holy life and have gone to their eternal reward will look out for us, if only we have the faith to ask them. Since his death in 1975 Josémaría Escrivá has been busy.

On record in Rome from all over the world are thousands of signed accounts of favors attributed to him: they range from inexplicable physical cures to marriages healed, addictions overcome, and jobs found. The majority attest to small, hidden miracles that come to mothers and fathers, sons and daughters in time of material, moral, or spiritual need.

The beatification of Monsignor Escrivá occurred in 1992. Officials at the Congregation for the Causes of the Saints have said much more about Josémaría Escrivá than quoted above, but this information is largely unknown to English-speaking audiences. So too the life of Blessed Josémaría is little known in the United States. Several episodes in his life would be the envy of many a screenwriter. It is worth recounting a few, if only in passing.

The early years of Opus Dei, before and during the Spanish Civil War, attest to an indomitable spirit intent on fulfilling God's will at all cost, even his own life and honor. The founder, among other things, was accused of being a heretic for proclaiming that God calls all people, not just the clergy and religious, to holiness.

During the frenzy of violence against the Church in the Civil War, the young Father Escrivá, despite the peril, preached itinerant retreats across Madrid, meeting small groups of people on the run, now in one house, later in another. A bounty was soon placed on his head; once, mistakenly thinking they had captured him, the militia hanged a man one morning from a tree in front of Escrivá's mother's house.

His escape on foot from war-torn Spain over the Pyrenees to Andorra in November 1937 was nothing short of harrowing. Anyone even suspected of attempting to flee faced summary execution. Hundreds perished in failed attempts. Blessed Josémaría and his companions spent nights on the run, days resting in caves and ravines. At the point of exhaustion, the emaciated priest prayed one evening for a sign that he should continue—upon which he found a gilded wooden rose from an altar of the Blessed

Virgin from a nearby bombed-out church. It was the special sign from Mary he had sought.

Beginning in the 1940s Blessed Josémaría was confronted with a new challenge: obtaining Vatican approval for Opus Dei so it could expand abroad. But the Church had never before encountered a phenomenon such as Opus Dei, and there were no adequate jurisdictional structures for it. Owing to its secular charism, a new legal structure would have to be created. But before that could happen, Opus Dei would have to accept a status that did not match its character.

It was not until the Second Vatican Council introduced Personal Prelatures into the life of the Church that an appropriate legal definition could be given to Opus Dei. Finally, in 1982, John Paul II established it as a Personal Prelature.

Naturally, the arduous legal path of Opus Dei caused the founder much suffering. Not everyone understood his message. As a good son of the Church his answer was always to pray and get others to pray; he never criticized. It was his firm conviction that God, in his own time, would bring about the eventual legal solution.

Others more knowledgeable than I have written at length about Personal Prelatures. Perhaps it is sufficient here to say that, as a Personal Prelature, Opus Dei is analogous to a diocese: it has its own prelate (currently Bishop Javier Echevarría, who resides in Rome), its own clergy, and lay faithful. The Prelature differs from a diocese in that the jurisdiction of the prelate extends over persons, not a circumscribed territory. His authority is only in what refers to the aims of the Prelature, namely the pursuit of a life of holiness in and by means of work and ordinary living. And like everyone else in the dioceses where they live, the members are subject to the local bishop in what pertains to all Catholics. The faithful of Opus Dei, like the faithful of a diocese, enjoy complete freedom within Church teaching in all social, political, and economic decisions. And, as in a diocese, there is pluralism and diversity in Opus Dei; the majority of members are of modest income, some poor, a few wealthy, some employed, others unemployed.

Once Opus Dei received its approval (though juridically inadequate) from the Vatican in 1947, Monsignor Escrivá dedicated himself to overseeing its development and expansion. From then on, his chief desire was to pass unnoticed, to work for Jesus without any human glory. Late in life he could say that he was merely "a stammering child," an instrument of God "worthy only for the waste basket," "a sinner madly in love with Jesus Christ."

Examples of his humility abound. The founder had no desire for titles, honors, or recognition. In the 1930s he asked permission of his confessor to make a promise that he never accept the dignity of being a bishop. His confessor replied that he could never grant such a request without the consent of the local bishop. After speaking with the bishop of Madrid, Father Josémaría wrote: "His excellency won't give me permission. I am really unhappy about this."

When the first priests of Opus Dei were ordained in 1944 he chose not to attend the ceremony, as he did not want to receive any congratulation. Then there is the story of the British bishop who asked the founder for a photo by which to remember him. In return he received a small image of a donkey. It was Monsignor Escrivá's way of referring to himself as an inept instrument in the hands of God. The anecdotes go on and on.

The media often surmise why the recent popes, including Pope John Paul II, have been favorably disposed toward Opus Dei. To John Paul II, who was an active participant in the Second Vatican Council, Opus Dei is a living manifestation, among others in the Church, of a key teaching of the council: the universal call to holiness and apostolate. "Yours is truly a great ideal," he said of Opus Dei in 1979. "From its very beginnings, it anticipated the theology of the laity that was later to characterize the Church of and after the Council."

A few years later John Paul spelled this out more clearly. In his homily at the beatification of Josémaría Escrivá in 1992 he spoke about the founder's zeal to remind all people that they are called from baptism to holiness of life. Then he said: "Christ calls everyone to become holy in the realities of everyday life. Hence, *work too is a means of personal holiness and apostolate* when it is lived in union with Jesus Christ, for the Son of God, in the incarnation, has united himself in a certain way with the whole reality of man and with the whole of creation [italics in original]."

Warming to the topic, the Pope continued: "In a society in which an unbridled craving for material things turns them into idols and a cause of separation from God, the new Beatus reminds us that these same realities, creatures of God and human industry, if used correctly for the glory of the Creator and the service of one's brothers and sisters *can be a way for men and women to meet Christ* [italics in original]."

This is also the reason people are attracted to Opus Dei. Men and women of all ages desire to understand their faith in relation to their ordinary day-to-day lives. They hunger for a spirituality that is appropriate to their condition as lay people. Many have tried other avenues for happiness, but they have been found wanting. They see in Opus Dei not only a faithfulness to Church teaching, but an institution dedicated to helping them discover on a personal basis how to incorporate their faith into their lives in a meaningful way. This, above all else, is the attraction of the message of Josémaría Escrivá.

John Paul II once said that Josémaría Escrivá is "counted among the great witnesses of Christianity." It is my hope and prayer that Vittorio Messori's investigation into Opus Dei goes a long way toward making his message better known and lived in the English-speaking world.

William Schmitt
Director of Communications, Prelature of Opus Dei
New Rochelle, NY
June 26, 1997

FOREWORD TO THE
AMERICAN EDITION

EVERY EUROPEAN WRITER IS naturally pleased to see a book of his published in the United States. The American market is the most important in the world, since it allows an author to reach a vast audience.

Two thousand years ago, anyone who had an important message to say wanted to say it in Rome, the capital of the Western world. This was also true with the rise of Christianity. Paul strove with all his strength to bring the Gospel to the heart of the Roman Empire. Today the role of the *Urbe,* the preeminent city, has passed on to the United States. An author who is unknown between the Atlantic and Pacific coasts runs the risk of being considered "provincial," even if he is well known elsewhere.

But along with my satisfaction as an author, there is also a certain cause for concern. Although American culture is rooted in Europe, it has taken on its own distinctive characteristics. Sensibilities and perspectives are quite different, even in the field of publishing. The foreign writer asks: "Will I be understood by this vast, and for us at times mysterious, American public?"

Since the subject of my book is such a Catholic reality, I trust these fears will prove groundless. "Catholic" in Greek of course means "universal." And in its long history that is about to enter the third millennium, the Catholic Church has shown its ability to speak to every culture and age. The Work founded by Blessed Josémaria Escrivá, following a divine inspiration, is an expression of authentic Catholic tradition and life. Therefore I hope that my attempt to explain Opus Dei will be understood by quite a diverse audience. Actually, this is more than just a hope, as readers of other translations of this book have already attested.

As Americans should appreciate, I have followed a pragmatic method in writing this book. It is not based on theories or hypotheses garnered solely from reading other authors. Rather, it is the work of a reporter who has spent his whole life working as a journalist. Although I am a Catholic, I knew very little about Opus Dei before tackling this book. What I write in the following pages I have learned by spending almost a year alongside people in Opus Dei and seeing how they actually live and work. I then tried to present my findings in the language of a journalist.

The original edition of this book was published at the request of Mondadori, an Italian publishing house that is one of the largest in Europe. Thus its status as a bestseller was attained in nonreligious bookstores, which are usually quite unenthusiastic about religious topics. I mention this because it shows how Opus Dei is news even outside of Catholic, or even Christian, settings.

As I foresaw in one of the book's early chapters, the strongest criticisms of the book have come from certain clerical milieus, while nonreligious reviewers have shown respect and interest. But in light of the Gospels, this is probably a positive sign.

CHAPTER ONE

A LETTER TO THE EDITORS

✝

We cease to hate when we cease to be ignorant.

—QUINTUS SEPTIMIUS TERTULLIANUS

When you set out on your apostolate, be assured that it is a matter of making people happy, very happy. Truth is inseparable from joy.

—JOSÉMARÍA ESCRIVÁ

OVER A YEAR AGO, I, a journalist, decided to investigate Opus Dei, or *la Obra* (the Work), to use its Castillian nickname.

In this investigation, there are few shades of gray. What I discovered is much more consoling or disturbing, much more promising or threatening, than most Catholics suspect. Certainly more than I suspected. And I speak not just of the present, but of the future. "We are only at the beginning of a great adventure" is commonly heard from many in the Work, with a disconcerting certainty that is neither arrogant nor righteous.

Opus Dei is an important reality in the Church. Founded in 1928, it presently numbers about 80,000 men and women in more than ninety nations—roughly 46,000 in Europe, 27,000 in the Americas, 4,000 in Oceania, and 1,000 in Africa, where it has been picking up speed. And it continues to grow.

Those in Opus Dei have often reminded me of the prophecy of the founder: "Opus Dei is like a sea without shores." Or in the words of one of its members: "It is not extravagant to say that a revolution is in the course of being carried out—with discretion, and usually in silence. The ecclesial importance of Opus Dei and its social extension are only now beginning to be felt. Only the passage of time will reveal its fullness."

To be more precise, those who believe in the Gospel and read it from a Catholic perspective take very seriously what Jesus said to Simon, son of Jonas: "You are Peter, and upon this Rock (*petra* = rock) I will found my Church, and the gates of hell will not prevail against it" (Mt. 16, 18).

And so the Church, built by the successors of Simon-called-Peter, will continue until the consummation of time, until the return of Christ in glory. What has *not* been written is what condition the Church will be in when it reaches that point.

But whatever the future of the Church, it seems safe to predict that Opus Dei will play a large role in it.

"Triumphalism" about the future is not an option for the discerning believer, given the unsettling remarks found in the same Gospel, such as in Luke 18.8: *"But will the Son of Man find any faith upon the earth?";* or in Matthew 24.11: *"Many false prophets will arise and deceive many: through the increase of iniquity, the love of many will grow cold";* or in St. Paul, 2 Titus, 2.3: *"First, in fact, apostasy will come, and the man of iniquity must be revealed, the son of perdition,"* and so on.

But whatever the future of the Church—whether it will grow or shrink—it seems safe to predict that Opus Dei will play a large role in it. I say this not as a prophet but based on the data I have collected, in the light of "trends," and in view of the constant and shifting factors that have governed twenty centuries of Christian history.

An old familiar paradox holds true: the groups assumed to be *avant garde,* those who think of themselves as the future, turn out to be the past. For some decades now, the "new" in ecclesiastical circles was represented by self-proclaimed progressivists—those who wanted not a dialogue but a real *fusion* with Marxism and, in general, with the so-called Left.

But with the fall of the Red Empire and its "scientific laws of history," that leftist brand of Catholicism, rather than being the prophet of the third millennium, has of a sudden become the survivor of a dusty nineteenth-century ideology.

Throughout these years of ecclesiastical debasement, Opus Dei remained faithful to Tradition and Teaching—that is, to the Magisterium of the Pope. And for this unshakable fidelity above all, the Work has been scorned as out of date; it has been distrusted as a kind of pre-Conciliar aberration.

Yet it is the "new" that suddenly plunged; it is the "old" that is methodically expanding, in numbers, in momentum, and in prestige.

All this is not of interest only to believers, because whatever happens in the Church has always had consequences for society as a whole. This is more true today than ever. As I review these pages, a simple slip and a broken bone of the Pope has put the worldwide media into a flurry of agitation.

I was asked to write this book to satisfy society's desire to know more about a "Work" which is defined as no less than a *"Work of God."* In the words of a prominent Opus Dei Spaniard, "The Work is a sensational theme for the press. It always sells very well."

But I have never chosen a theme merely because of its popularity or because it promised a big profit. And so, when I refused at first, it was not through any virtue on my part. My refusal arose from necessity. Life is short, one's powers are limited; it is better to use them to investigate and reflect upon more profound queries. A book is years in the making (if one tries to write it as

God wants it written); no amount of money or fame could possibly compensate for the grind, tedium, and fatigue of the solitary work of writing were it not for some compulsion. And so, for a time, the urge to investigate Opus Dei was simply not in me.

But, in due course, the fortunes of my life's voyage brought me to a Christian harbor I had not foreseen. And I am happy here. And if it is God's will, I will not leave.

In the Church, I have never belonged to any groups, associations, movements, confraternities, orders, organizations, or "works." I appreciate them all, I rejoice at their existence, and I hope they prosper and multiply. I look on them as the new shoots that sprout spontaneously in every generation from the venerable tree of the Church. The Church rightly calls herself "catholic," that is, "universal." For two millennia, the Church has opened her doors to the most diverse temperaments, vocations, and personal histories. As my old friend Henri Fesquet (whose *Le Monde* revolutionized the world of religious news) once told me: "The Church is the largest and most diverse zoo in the world—it has a niche for every conceivable species of animal."

As a Catholic, then, but as one unattached to any particular group, I knew as much about Opus Dei as could be expected. I thought of it in terms of reserve, austerity, seriousness, solid preparation (both professional and theological), prestige, socioeconomic influence—even the hint of a personal cult of the founder, the (now) Blessed Josémaría Escrivá, or as the members refer to him, "our father" *(Nuestro Padre)*. On a few occasions, I spent some time at a public get-together in the Castello di Urio, an eighteenth-century mansion on the shore of Lake Como, which men and women of the Work use for their formational activities, especially of university students and professionals.

I was at ease. I experienced the "Opus Dei style": the best education, good taste in clothing ("mystics with the right kind of tie," as somebody said), an absence of clericalism, a lay casualness.

And no confusion between true, evangelical poverty and the squalor so commonly imposed on guests, or the equation of Christian radicalism with carelessness and bad taste.

In a Catholicism where these days a church building is often deemed more Christian the closer it resembles a garage, I appreciated the sober but attractive richness of the chapel (or "oratory," as they prefer to call it)—modern, but with ancient lines, and built with the conviction that it is a sin to be stingy with beauty in places where God is worshipped, that plastic, aluminum, and concrete may be just fine for industrial buildings, but not for a church.

I admired the solid, traditional pews with kneelers, and, new to me, the small electric lights for individual spiritual reading. I also admired them for not giving in to the fashion of forcing the faithful to sit on the floor on pillows, an ecumenical gesture expressing a "more adult" Christianity. And no stale odors from the kitchen or refectory, no modern encrustations or faded posters with political or ecological themes, where paintings of the old masters were wont to hang.

For my professional work or for personal reasons, I have spent much time in such religious places; it is the look of many of them in the twilight of the orders and congregations that were once glorious. Their appearance does not attract anyone who is not already "in."

But this is not the case in the Centers of Opus Dei—not only in the beautiful Castello di Urio, a kind of showcase, but to differing degrees in all the other Centers of the Work I eventually visited while making this investigation. Someone told me that Blessed Escrivá often said that he had to know the "hand" of his sons and daughters, making sure that the floor shone like a mirror, that the curtains were immaculate, that the furniture was free of dust; cleanliness and good taste didn't cost a thing, apart from the effort of those who lived in the place and created the right atmosphere for spirituality.

My contacts with the Work and my awareness of these matters were of the common sort: superficial, and limited to the externals. But it was not irrelevant—today, it is less irrelevant than before, and it will be even less so tomorrow. The wisdom of the ancient Church—a wisdom seemingly lost in ideological dreams—knew well that the beauty, or at least the *decorum* of Catholic environments, of the buildings used for worship in the monasteries attracted people and spoke to them of God.

Keeping in mind what I knew (or *didn't* know) about this institution, let me tell you an anecdote.

One evening some years back, waiting to board the last plane to Milan, I saw the unmistakable and good-humored face of that kindly and shrewd Lombard priest, Rev. Luigi Giussani, founder and president of *Communione e Liberazione.* After we exchanged greetings, Don Gius, as his followers call him, told me he had enjoyed a visit that morning with Msgr. del Portillo, the prelate, or highest official, of Opus Dei, and the successor of Blessed Josémaría Escrivá. (Bishop Alvaro del Portillo died on March 3, 1994, and on April 20 Pope John Paul II approved Msgr. Javier Echevarría as the new prelate of Opus Dei.)

"You know," he said, taking me by the elbow, "we are the guerrillas, the irregulars, the rock-throwers. We do our part, and sometimes really stir something up. But those people in the Work, they have the tanks: they are well armored with rubber-coated treads. Nobody has heard of them yet, but they're here, believe me. And we'll be talking about them more and more, you'll see."

A detachment of tanks, then, to be added to the already heterogeneous company of passengers on the ship that the Church is and has always been. It is a fine detachment, made up of people in neat uniforms and with bright, well-polished equipment. Well instructed, too, and obedient to their generals—unobjectionable. But it is still only one battalion among many, one way among many ways, attractive to some, off-putting to others, to try to live the

Gospel in today's world. The spirituality of Monsignor Escrivá is one among the many that have appeared through the ages of Catholicism: Carmelite, Dominican, Franciscan, Jesuit, Salesian, Passionist, and so forth.

Or so I thought. But I don't think so any more, as I have been suggesting. And this because I have done my utmost to try to understand this "thing" which seems so small from the outside. At any rate, here is the dossier. I am not a first-time author; I have seen, heard, and reported everything. And I can foresee certain reactions. The most agitated ones will probably not come from rabid anticlericals but from various "good Catholics." I use the adjective "good" without irony. At the outset, I always assume good faith, and it was Don Escrivá himself who confided that the worst persecution came from "good people" in the Church herself.

> *The spirituality of Monsignor Escrivá is only one among the many that have appeared through the ages of Catholicism.*

Among those who will find this report too favorable, the most generous will suspect me of naiveté, of not having grasped the hidden "deception" that lies behind certain healthy appearances of Opus Dei.

Others, less genteel, will say this is not an investigation but rather an apology, and a poorly disguised one at that—probably commissioned. And if not money, then prejudice, or sectarian fanaticism, has moved my fingers to play the tune.

I have no reply other than the one journalists always use: I am reporting facts, not impressions. What I write is always and exclusively based on what I have seen myself or what I have read in official and unofficial sources. If I am contradicted, I expect it to be on the basis of the same sources. If anyone is in a position to do it better, I will be glad to read the outcome. What I have discovered, and understood, after a good deal of rumination is here.

I have sought, above all, to understand primarily for myself what this Work *is:* How does it *function?* What are the personal and institutional *mainsprings* that drive it?

The quotation at the beginning was not casually chosen: it comes from an ancient Christian writer who had a particular regard for *caritas:* "We cease to hate when we cease to be ignorant." Along the same lines, he said that if the person wanted to keep distrusting something or someone, he should take great care to avoid learning anything about that thing or person. I don't think the Work—or even the mythical Mafia of Don Escrivá—can escape this rule. At all events, the reader must decide for himself.

"We cease to hate when we cease to be ignorant."— Tertullian

As for my personal perspective, I think being a believer helped rather than hindered my understanding of the nature of Opus Dei. It would help to understand any Christian institution, beginning with the Church herself. I attempt to explain why in Chapter 7, "A Religious Reality." Any religious experience can be legitimately judged only by adequate concepts, and that means by religious categories.

It is the profound conviction of its nearly 80,000 members from all nations of the world that Opus Dei is, above all, a spiritual reality and an experience of faith. If this is not taken into account, we risk not understanding it at all. Or, worse, we risk misunderstanding it.

CHAPTER TWO
A "DARK TALE"

OPUS DEI. A PERFECT name, with a good ominous sound: a writer of crime novels couldn't have done better.

When Mussolini wanted to set up the secret police, his first priority was to think up a name, a name that would strike fear and anxiety in men.

He finally settled on OVRA, which his expert advisors told him had just the right sound. Apparently, it was only later that words were invented to fit the acronym; historians still debate its meaning. What mattered to the Duce was only that the name have a sinister sound to whisper into terrified ears.

And then there is Opus Dei. Even beyond the sound is the meaning itself: *Opus Dei* in Latin means "Work of God." Isn't there a hint of Luciferian pride here? Some people have thought so, even in the Church. "These Spaniards are all megalomaniacs.

In the sixteenth century, Ignatius, a Basque of Loyola, founded a religious order and called it the *Societas Jesu* [the Society of Jesus]. As if they alone were the servants of Christ and as if they alone had Him as their 'Captain'! In the twentieth century, an Aragonese of Barbastro, Escrivá, has gone even further: his foundation is called, simply, the 'Work of God,' which is like saying the 'Divine Work.' This is worse than saying, 'God is on our side.' It is pretentious to identify something created by a human being, however saintly, with something created by God Himself. Nobody has ever pushed his conceit so far...."

This accusation has dogged Opus Dei almost from the beginning, since 1930 to be exact, when it was first given that name in a casual remark by the young Father Escrivá's confessor. The members have a reply, of course: they say that a Work of God is a sign not of pride but of humility. To explain, they point to the origins and theological outlook of the Work in question. This is an important point, but we must put it off for now.

The constant preoccupation of Escrivá was to preserve at all costs the lay nature of his followers.

To continue with names. The names of the members also have an ominous sound: *numeraries, supernumeraries, associates.* These unusual titles were chosen by the founder himself, to distinguish his group from ecclesiastical tradition: the religious orders. The constant preoccupation of Escrivá (and one of the main issues I want to clarify in this book) was to preserve at all costs the lay nature of his followers, in reality as well as in appearance. This can be seen not only in the names of the members, but also in the names of the Centers.

At Number 75 Viale Bruno Buozzi in the Parioli district, behind a solid but somewhat anonymous facade of the sixteenth and seventeenth centuries, stands the labyrinthine complex built during the thirty years the Blessed Escrivá lived in Rome and where his successor, the prelate, now resides. This title signifies the acting head of what is known in official language as the "Personal Prelature of the Holy Cross and Opus Dei."

This headquarters, from which the bishop-prelate holds the reins of the worldwide organization, has no religious name, nor has it been placed under the protection of some saint or title of Mary, as is customary for Catholic orders, congregations, and institutions. Nothing of the sort. This "mother-house" has been given the lay name of Villa Tevere (Tiber Villa).

Behind it rise other buildings from which come the direction, also worldwide, of the female branch: again, the name has no hint of devotionalism but sounds almost bureaucratic: Villa Sachetti, the name of the street where the buildings are located.

How about the university residence and a residence of women located in the elegant little Plaza Liberty across the Tiber? No great leap of imagination is required to see that it gets its name from the two lovely trees that sway in its yard: the Villa delle Palme.

The building that houses the Espozione Universale di Roma (EUR), where I was put up as a guest while making my investigations in Rome and its environs, is the anonymous-sounding Residenza Universitaria Internazionale. And the one in Palermo? Also a Residenza Universitaria, but Mediterranean. And so it goes throughout the world. I traveled around and consulted lists and internal publications, and I never found a house, a Center, an apostolic work of Opus Dei that had a religious-sounding name.

The large Center of professional formation for young workers in the Tiburtine Quarter of Rome (of which I will speak later), for which Opus Dei provides official doctrinal and spiritual orientation, is called ELIS, an acronym for Educazione, Lavoro, Istruzione, Sport. Religion is not even mentioned: it is included in these other realities.

In the twenties in Italy a group inspired by the Franciscan priest Agostino Gemelli founded a university which was not only called "Catholic" but "Of the Sacred Heart." The university of Opus Dei at Pamplona, by contrast, was given the simple name of the University of Navarre. And this despite the unambiguous language of its charter, or *Ideario:* "[The University of Navarre] is a corporate work of Opus Dei, and the spirit of the latter animates its life and activities, nourishing, in those who are part of it, a love for the Church, the Pope, and the Magisterium, with full respect for freedom of conscience, in the unity of a coherent, Christian life, as well as in the requisite practice of the human virtues."

This deliberate avoidance of religious-sounding names feeds the continuing suspicions of "masonic secrecy," or simply some clandestine criminal activity.

Don Bosco, a saint of vigor, intelligence, and inflexible determination in pursuit of his goal, has several points in common with Blessed Escrivá. In the nineteenth century, he likewise thought up names for his followers that differed from the traditional ones. The head of the Salesians was not called the "Superior General," as in other religious orders, but the "Rector Major" *(rettor maggiore).* For local government, the provinces were called "inspectories" *(ispettorie).* And the Salesian priests avoided the name of "father" and called themselves "don," like the secular priests. Like other communities of men and women, the Salesian society arose in a century unmatched for the number of religious foundations— persecution has always, it seems, been good for the Church and for Christians. But behind the lay facade was the traditional religious reality, cloaked by the needs of the times.

But Opus Dei is not like this. Its founder always said, "We love and respect the religious [the brothers, monks, sisters, members of congregations and institutions who have taken the three traditional vows of poverty, chastity, and obedience], but we are not religious, and no authority on earth, or in the Church, can force us to become religious."

This is an important point, and at first it may be disconcerting. "These people say they want to live to the full their religious convictions, yet they insist they are not to be called religious. Are they then lay people?" Yes, precisely.

Here we are dealing with a purely linguistic matter, rather than a theological or canonical one. Names like numerary and supernumerary and associate (unlike names like novice, postulant, brother, or sister) have been taken from the worlds of the Spanish academy and government. In effect, a numerary in Spanish and Latin-American universities corresponds to an ordinary professor, and the title refers to the level of the civil service.

There is also an unfortunate coincidence—the word *numerario*, when used as a noun and not as an adjective, means "the sum total of paper and coin currency" (*cf. the word numismatist,* "coin collector"). This unintended reference to money is a particularly dangerous word-play in this instance, considering the suspicion that great wealth and obscure financial maneuvers take place within Opus Dei. The word *numerary,* with its etymology (*cf.* Latin *numerus,* "number") also hints at the unsettling anonymity of a very exclusive club, of a secret society where the members do not have names but numbers, or code names.

And so, it is one thing to refer to a "Franciscan brother" or a "Jesuit father" or a "member of Catholic Action"; it is quite another to refer to a *numerario de la Obra.* Names are important, especially these days, when the appearance, the *look,* even in language, contains so much more of the reality, of the essence of something. And yet it is not the name Opus Dei nor the names of its members that have created the atmosphere of suspicion, distrust, or aversion. These have only been nourished and confirmed by the names.

The creation of Escrivá, it seems, achieved a permanent position in something called "obscure forces," "hidden powers," "invisible string-pullers." The obsession with secret plots and conspiracies has been a constant of history, but it appears to have assumed more importance, even delirious proportions, in our times which pride themselves on being so rational. It is not by chance that a new specialty in journalism is what might be called "behind-the-scenes-ism": everything that happens, everything bad, that is, must be researched to discover "what's behind it," with free rein given to the most bizarre guesses. It is an unquestionable dogma that there is *always* someone behind everything.

The truth is, the age-old belief in the devil was a kind of safety valve which probably deflected as many calamities as it created. Everything bad in humanity in an individual could be attributed to that malevolent power. And it was fought against, above all, by prayer, exorcism, and self-denial. (In contrast, the attempted manipulation of history by "the majority" has been much more violent: the few months of the Jacobin Terror of 1793 or of Stalin's purges saw infinitely more victims than all the centuries of the Inquisition put together.) A further tactic was to keep surveillance on those with whom the Enemy, the Father of Lies, had his business, and if necessary, to bring them to trial and isolate them.

But now that this belief has disappeared, there is still the problem: who is to blame for a world that insists on going off-track, despite all the solemn statements of lay moralists, the blueprints for earthly paradise of intellectuals, the utopias of visionaries, the ideologies meant to redeem us, the reforms, the reforms of the reforms, the revolutions? There ought to be someone to blame for the evil in the world!

This, then, begets the obsession with the plot, with the fifth column, those who secretly pull the strings of history. This is why the bourgeoisie of the French Revolution cut off the heads of the aristocrats, why the Leninists shot the bourgeoisie, why the Nazis mass-murdered Jews, why the liberals blamed the communists for every crime. In these last two centuries of alienation from tradition and from the Christian faith, the role of the devil, of his minions and witches, has been foisted onto someone else—with dangerous, and often quite bloody, consequences.

Thus demonization of the Work has become an international phenomenon, common to the entire West, but I will restrict myself here to events in Italy, selecting a few examples from thousands.

Autumn, 1992: the Congress of International Socialism at the Hague. Hunted by Milanese authorities for corrupting his party, and realizing that he would soon be forced to step down as secretary of the PSI (Italian Socialist Party), Bettino Craxi lets off steam with reporters. He explains he is "the victim of secret conspiracies" and writes as follows: "They are talking about freemasonry. And what is Opus Dei? All you have to do is turn around and somebody whispers, 'That guy's from Opus Dei.' These are the true secrets. But I am reacting...."

Spring 1993: This time, the authorities are going after the Grand Orient of Italy itself, suspecting it of corruption, various illicit practices, and subversive plots. Served by subpoenas, the Grand Master of Masons denounces the same "secret conspiracies": "It is a plot of Opus Dei, the true, omnipresent, all-powerful, secret society. They go after us Masons to divert attention from the *Opusdeisti.* "

Summer 1993: In Milan and Rome car bombs explode at night, killing people and destroying famous monuments. In an "exclusive interview" one of the authoritative news magazines reveals that one lead points to Opus Dei (defined as "a powerful political and financial arm of the Holy See"), that the Work commissioned the attacks on the Lateran, the Pope's cathedral, and against other venerable religious buildings to send a warning to the Vatican not to keep its distance from the corrupt Social Democrat Party. According to another "school of thought," the Work was not the planter of the bombs but the intended victim!

In January 1993, the *Economist,* one of the more serious and informed journals in the world, published a "guide" to good networks, including various orders of Freemasonry, exclusive orders of knights, and more or less secret societies.

And of course Opus Dei is here. It earned the ranking of a 5 (the highest score) for "power of conviction," a 4 for "organization," and a 3 for "secrecy." And finally, it received a 1—the lowest possible score—for "exclusivity": a confirmation from an unexpected source of something the Work constantly claims. And this claim is that any man or woman, as long as he or she is called by God, can become a member with full rights, without regard to social status.

Another detail in the *Economist* article deserves mention. It states quite seriously that "strangers can discover members of Opus Dei by observing small tell-tale signs." For instance? "A whiff of Atkinson's cologne, the favorite of Escrivá, is a good giveaway."

In short, a day does not pass that the fax machine of the Office of Information of the Personal Prelature doesn't send out corrections and qualifications to journals which have attributed practically everything to Opus Dei: from assassinations and slayings to bank accounts (it is now almost automatic to see the "gnomes of Opus Dei" behind every important, and possibly crooked, financial operation); from the unexpected death of Pope John Paul I to military coups in South America. Not to speak, of course, of the continuous accusations of collusion with the regime of the late Franco of Spain in pursuit of power and money.*

In February 1986, some on the Italian Left (stirred by a hard-hitting campaign of the press led by the weekly *L'Espresso*) demanded that the law of 1982 "against secret societies" be used against Opus Dei. This law had been passed in great haste to stop the scandal of the "Propaganda 2" (the "P2"). This legally recognized Masonic lodge was part of the leading "family" of Italian Freemasonry known as the "Palace Justinians."

The minister of the interior, Oscar Luigi Scalfaro, responded to the allegations with an extended inquiry that even involved the Vatican. Finally, on November 24, 1986, the future president of the Republic of Italy appeared before the chamber with a bulky dossier on the whole issue. In an unprecedented move, Scalfaro had the text privately printed and distributed to the members of Parliament to facilitate their following the complicated argument. Indeed, it anticipated this report: it was a true "investigation into Opus Dei."

But the journalists who had spent months calling the Work a secret political conspiracy were able in just a few lines to discredit Scalfaro's text.

In a single column, they charged that the government had disappointed the hopes for sincerity, justice, and clean dealings and insinuated that the affair was doomed, given a "bigot" like Scalfaro as minister of the interior. And there were allusions to the interference of a foreign state (Vatican City) into Italian affairs, in order to deflect, silence, and obstruct judicial and administrative attempts to confront this "powerful political lobby." (It is interesting to note

"At this point there is nothing left but to draw the conclusions: Opus Dei is not secret, neither de jure nor de facto."

that the president of the committee, who was ultimately responsible for the government's response, was none other than Bettino Craxi.)

Here, unabridged, is the conclusion of Scalfaro's report, which he read that day in Parliament: "At this point there is nothing left but to draw the conclusions: Opus Dei is not secret neither *de jure* nor *de facto;* the duties of obedience (to which its members are called) are exclusively concerned with matters of spirituality; they have no other rights or duties than those prescribed in the *Codex iuris particularis* (Code of Particular Law) of the Work, and these too are strictly spiritual in nature; there is no duty or right in the older canonical rule of the institute that has not been allowed for by the new one, and has survived in the institution of the Prelature. Consequently, neither the government nor the minister of the interior in particular can legitimately assume initiatives with regard to

Opus Dei or prepare investigations or verifications of censure against it. Indeed (on the basis of the precepts of the Constitution, and the fundamental rights of liberty which the Constitution guarantees; on the basis of the obligation of Concordat—solemnly reaffirmed in the Accord of Villa Madame of 1982—with full respect for the principle of sovereignty and independence of the Catholic Church; on the basis of the statutes which govern the Prelature; on the basis, finally, of the statements of the Holy See, which, as stated, represent its official position on the matter, and are binding on the Prelature itself), these governmental investigations and certifications, not being able to justify in any element of fact any action that would strengthen even the most meager suspicion, would be equivalent to an inadmissible compromise of the citizen's right to liberty, and in an equally inadmissible interference of the State into the internal order of the Church. The religious peace of the Church (a peace which the Assembly indicated to be of supreme value, when it discussed and voted on Article 7 of the Constitutional Charter) is realized with respect to the letter and spirit of this norm, in an essential context of truth, the unique foundation of justice and peace."

All this notwithstanding, the reputation of the Work as an "occult group" continues to add spice to an obscure event. As just one example: the international press saw the direct hand of some numerary, or at least of some order issued from the "den" at Viale Bruno Buozzi, behind the hanging of the banker Roberto Calvi under Blackfriar's Bridge in London.

Opus Dei's policy for dealing with this sort of thing was set in motion by the founder. The attacks began when it was nothing but a small group of young men around a young priest, in the 1930s in pre-Civil War Spain. The strategy consisted in not replying with counterattacks. As one recent study states, "There is not a single book by the Work itself or by any of its many thousand members that is written *against* anyone or anything."

The idea, rather, is to explain, to seek to dissipate the confusions, and to clarify what Opus Dei is and how it functions. And if the "others" do not understand, the members respond as the founder taught them, in three words: *pray, smile, forgive (rezar, sonreir, perdonar)*.

Monsignor Escrivá liked to recall the words of the Gospel, "There is no servant higher than his master. If He is to be called Beelzebub, whom they have attacked with so much calumny, how can it be different for His followers?" At the conclusion of a press conference in 1967 in Pamplona—possibly the only one in his life—he bade the journalists farewell. "I don't want to know what you are going to write. If it is the truth, God will reward you. If it is not the truth, I will pray for you. So either way, you win...." Nor does it appear that Opus Dei has lost anything, given its steady growth, by these attacks. In fact, such attacks can even strengthen the resolve of a group. But this is not encouraged. Opus Dei wants to be open to the apostolate, with its members living in society like normal citizens, not like members of a sect who are happy to be "persecuted."

The attacks, suspicions, and false inferences don't come only from lay or secular circles, which set themselves against a Catholic world marshaled to defend Opus Dei from the ill-will of unbelievers. Rather, the suspicions of and the attacks on Opus Dei since its infancy have emanated more often than not from ecclesiastical circles, especially from Spanish religious orders acting more out of anxiety and fear of novelty than out of malevolence; the "dark tale," in fact, had its origin in clerical circles. All the arguments that persist to this day were first developed by Catholics.

As an example: there is a relatively recent (1992) reference work, one of those quasi-official publications that tend to be moderate and fairly objective. This particular work is in Italian, edited by a prominent Catholic from the third German edition, and frequently used in the Church today. It is the *Dizionario storico del cristianesimo* by Andresen-Denzler. Opus Dei, a reality in today's Catholicism, impressive even if judged only quantitatively, has been given half the space of an article on "Josephinism" (a problem of the eighteenth century) and the same amount of space as the "Beguines" (an extinct phenomenon of the early fourteenth century). The article on Opus Dei warns that it is a "traditionalist in matters of religion" and goes on to describe the Work as "always subject to bitter polemics," adding that "some think highly of the vital force and spirituality of this 'lay elite of Catholicism,' while others characterize the institution as a proponent of 'restoration,' which seeks the answer to all problems of private and public life in faith alone, and therefore denies the autonomy of particular fields of culture." Some Christians, it seems, consider it a fault to place faith at the center of life and to seek guidance, or at least orientation, from their faith.

This authoritative *Historical Dictionary of Christianity*—objective and praiseworthy in other respects—concludes the article as follows: "Its close connections with Franco's regime, and its sympathy for the right-wing, have raised suspicions." There the article ends. And so, with this information presented as fact, the Work has been dispensed with, in a work used by lay Catholics in theological schools, and officially consulted in the formation of priests. Similar misinformation can also be found in the *New Columbia Encyclopedia* (Columbia University Press, 1993) and in the *Encyclopedia Americana* (Grolier's, 1991).

To explain the diffidence, if not the hostility, of the Catholic world toward the Work (the world from which the secular world gets its cues), people always refer to an episode that took place thirty years ago.

It is recalled again and again that the great Hans Urs von Balthasar, the Swiss Jesuit who became a secular priest, took a critical position against the Work. Von Balthasar is among the greatest and most talked-about Catholics of the century. During the pontificate of John XXIII, von Balthasar was suspected of excessive "openness" and was not invited to participate in the activities of the Vatican Council's theological committees. After the council, the situation was reversed, and the presumed progressivist was changed into a conservative—not always accurately, some believe.

Later, von Balthasar became a favorite son of John Paul II, who in 1984 gave him a kind of Vatican Nobel Prize, the Pope Paul VI award, and in 1988 named him cardinal (the great scholar died a few days before leaving for Rome to receive his cardinal's hat).

A great theologian, a man of extraordinary erudition, and a priest who led a vigorously Christian life, von Balthasar had some peculiar, perhaps even contradictory, characteristics.

I myself once experienced great difficulties through his unsettling behavior—the story is told only because I think it will help clarify the point and not out of a wish to reduce all questions to autobiography. In the autumn of 1985, he gave me an interview that took up two entire pages of the daily Catholic journal *Avvenire* and provoked a great fuss throughout the Church. It was translated into various languages and printed as a brochure. Even Pope John Paul II, I was told, had a version translated into Polish: he liked the interview because the Swiss theologian defended him from Hans Küng, another Swiss theologian, whose attacks at that time were particularly virulent.

A few days afterward, Balthasar, without warning, retracted some of the major statements he had made in my interview. He did this in one of the most authoritative German daily newspapers, the *Frankfurter Allgemeine Zeitung.* There was an immediate uproar everywhere. Just as immediate was a request from me to him and to the persons responsible for copies of the cassette tapes of the interview to confirm that the theologian had been quoted with absolute fidelity. And just as immediate was the testimony of the director of *Avvenire,* who had been present at the original interview which had taken place at Basel, confirming that it had been accurately reported.

This was followed by private letters from von Balthasar (I still have them), the last of which concluded with some disturbing words: "I understand very well your bitterness and I confess I was surprised by what you say about my words on your tapes.... It is my fault.... I ask you, please, to bury this affair, which has caused so much trouble for everyone."

The story is told only because this great man of learning seems to have had some peculiar oscillations as well with regard to Opus Dei. It is significant, because some of his books are of fundamental importance for the Church of today.

In November 1963, von Balthasar published an article on "Integrism" in the *Neue Zürcher Zeitung,* a small Swiss journal, now defunct, with a small circulation. The article was reprinted the following month in the authoritative Vienna theological review *Wort und Wahrheit.*

The article mentioned Opus Dei, defining it as "an integrist concentration of power in the Church." According to the theologian, the central motivation of "integrism" is to try "imposing the spiritual with worldly means." The article followed one in which von Balthasar wrote critically of Teilhard de Chardin and opposed clerical "progressivism." He thus condemned both the ecclesiastical "Left" and "Right." In the latter category he placed the Work, which, as he later confessed, he hardly was aware of at the time— the Work had barely begun to take its first steps in Switzerland. His negative judgment was based almost entirely on some analyses of a few points of Monsignor Escrivá's work, *The Way,* which he judged at the time as not being deep enough spiritually for its worldwide pretensions.

It was easy for members of Opus Dei to show irrefutably (juxtaposing the original and the quoted version) that the text of *The*

Way had been manipulated: some phrases had been "torn" from the context, others had been unfairly joined, still others had been shorn of their explanations. In sum, it was a case of what Joseph Fouche, or someone just like him, had said: "Give me somebody's written text, and I could make enough cuts and changes in it to send him to the guillotine."

But now, after thirty years, it is no longer a debatable matter. Yet it was brought up once again in an attempt to prevent Monsignor Escrivá's beatification, discussed below. The argument ran: how can Opus Dei not be "integrist," or "of the Right," or "as powerful as it is hidden," when nobody less than a theologian friend of the Pope decided to keep Opus Dei at arm's length?"

As a journalist who tries to exercise his profession, I undertook to examine the dossier of the entire case.

The dossier provided a surprising... *absence.* The famous article appeared as stated in 1963, and its author died in 1988, still intellectually active. In those twenty-five years, in the hundreds if not thousands of pieces bearing his signature, von Balthasar not only did not write or speak a single word against Opus Dei, but he even retracted what he had said. For example, in 1984 he wrote as follows to a priest of the Prelature: "Some decades ago, I criticized *The Way* (but not Opus Dei!), because it seemed to me to be spiritually insufficient for so great an ambition. Since that time, I have not said a word against Opus Dei."

Two years later, on December 19, 1986, while making the same point to Hans Thomas, another member of the Work, he confessed, "At that time [in 1963] I didn't know any members of the Work."

But more significant than these private documents is some public testimony of 1979 which has never been cited by any critic, as justice would seem to require. But it is fair to point out that it would be difficult for anyone to cite, since the publication in which it ought to appear refuses to publish it.

The paper in question is considered by many as the most authoritative daily of Switzerland, the *Neue Zürcher Zeitung,* distinguished for its tradition of lay radicalism. Von Balthasar addressed a letter to the directing editor of the newspaper, who refused to publish it. The theologian also sent a signed copy to the directors of the Work in Switzerland, who have it in their archives. In the letter, von Balthasar states: "In the *Neue Zürcher* of January 1979, there appeared a violent attack on the activities of Opus Dei in Zürich, a piece which does not seem worthy of a daily newspaper which has received the Erasmus prize—a prize named for Erasmus, the great conciliator! In this article I am cited as the principal witness against the organization. Fortunately, the author has given precise reference to an article of mine which appeared in 1963 (in a journal which is no longer published), but has left out the fact that in reality that article was a review of *The Way,* a work written by the founder of Opus Dei. That article of mine did not make a judgment on the work of Monsignor Escrivá as a whole (which at the time was not as accessible in all its original spiritual depth, as it is today). At the time, in 1963, my impression was only that the statements and exhortations contained in *The Way* did not seem an adequate basis for so influential an organization, of worldwide expansion. For lack of concrete information, I am not in a position to deliver a judgment on Opus Dei as it now is, and yet I am certain that many of the accusations (including those which the article in your paper advances against the religious instruction carried out by the members of Opus Dei) are simply false and anticlerical."

After reading such a letter it would seem more prudence is needed to discredit the Work than by saying that "[e]ven the theologian most admired by Pope Wojtyla has cautioned Catholics about it."

And there is still the final document of the affair to consider. It is probably one of von Balthasar's last articles, which appeared posthumously in the July 1988 issue of the journal *Diakonia*. The translated title is "Integrism Today," a reprise of the theme treated in the celebrated text of 1963. It is a full reexamination of the phenomenon which he had seen exemplified in Opus Dei twenty-five years before. But in this theological "last testament" there is not the slightest reference to Opus Dei—nothing, not a single direct or indirect reference, not a single word.

The only viable conclusion is that there was a change of opinion—something noted more than once in von Balthasar's long and passionate lifetime of scholarship.

All this aside, on May 17, 1992, Rome, the city of traffic jams, had its "longest day"—a practically total blockage of traffic. On certain streets and at certain times it was impossible to get anywhere even by foot. And this was because of an invasion of around 300,000 to 400,000 persons from all parts of the world, by every possible means of transportation, in order to be present at the beatification of the Venerable Josémaría Escrivá de Balaguer y Albas, which took place in

On May 17, 1992, Rome had its "longest day"— 300,000 to 400,000 persons at Pope John Paul II's beatification of Josémaría Escrivá.

St. Peter's Plaza, and at the hands of John Paul II himself.

Bernini, the architect of St. Peter's, would have been dizzy at the sight: the 284 columns and their 140 statues of saints and apostles—designed to embrace the largest crowd imaginable—were not enough. It is possibly the only time this has occurred in the more than three centuries of the Piazza's history.

Looking at a photograph taken from the cupola, one sees that every corner of the huge baroque expanse is packed. And this is no mere scattering of people. The whole space is thickly covered in ordered sections, divided by lanes open only to servers and first aid personnel. And then the orderly sea of heads stretches out along the Via della Conciliazione, almost reaching the Tiber in the distance.

An impressive vision of tranquil power, of self-confidence; a festive atmosphere under the Italian sun, in honor of a Spaniard, but in ranks so orderly and compact that it evoked something more northern, even Teutonic. The atmosphere was one of discipline, or rather, self-discipline. And the immense rally was not there to declare war, but peace; not to sow hatred, but love; not to get revenge, but to express gratitude.

It took a long time to reach that day, to hear a Pope with the apostolic authority entrusted to him add *El Padre* to the list of the blessed, to be able to bring together that massive crowd from the four corners of the world, a crowd both orderly and jubilant. A long, hard battle had to be fought before Opus Dei could attain this honor. More than anywhere, this battle was fought within the Church.

Behind the clerical scenes, there were numerous maneuvers and countermaneuvers to intimidate the Pope himself, to make him postpone the beatification, if nothing else.

One of many newspaper reports should suffice: "When it was announced (in December 1991) that the solemn beatification of the founder of Opus Dei was to take place on May 17 of the following year, the matter instantly became news. Beatifications usually make very small impact on the newspapers, even Catholic ones. But now, for the first time in the modern world, groups went into action to disqualify the process, to cast doubts on the person named for beatification, and consequently, on the person of the Pope himself, and on the objectivity and legitimacy of his decision to go ahead with the ceremony. A lot of 'firepower' was deployed, with persistent support, to block, delay, or at least spoil the celebration planned for May 17, 1992."

Some even went so far as to threaten a possible schism from Rome, considering "the glorification of Opus Dei, in the person of its founder, to be intolerable and scandalous." Others proposed a peculiar either-or alternative to the Pope: "Why Escrivá, *yes,* and

Pope John XXIII, *no?*" (In ecclesiastical language, this suggests that the Church is rewarding *restaurazione* as opposed to *aggiornamento*). "Why," the protest continues, "did it take so long for other candidates and take only seventeen years for this Spaniard?"

There was even controversy about the miracle, which is required by the Church as a sort of *imprimatur* of the holiness of the candidate to be raised to the altars. These divine signs of approval are required for the leap from "venerable" to "blessed" (and later, for the elevation to "saint"). The "healing inexplicable by the state of contemporary science"—the official formula—was certified, in the usual way, by a group of reputable experts who had been named to the Vatican Congregation for the Causes of the Saints. For some of the tests, the Work had summoned as its representative experts (*periti di parte*) two specialists from the University of Navarre, chosen particularly for the scientific equipment at their disposal. This collaboration with the educational institution, of which the prelate is the chancellor, was attacked, giving talk of "manipulation," of a "false miracle," with the Pope represented as the victim of a lobby of cheats and swindlers. These critics pretended not to be aware that the specialists had participated only in the information-gathering phase as representative experts and that their appraisal, as in every process, was subject to the autonomous and impartial judgment of the experts of the Vatican congregation.

This may sound harsh to those who do not understand how hot theological anger can grow. But it is not completely bad that some people still take such religious questions seriously in a world that appears to believe in nothing. Nor do such confrontations blur the recognition that all those in the Church are still brothers in what unites them—their common faith. In the Catholic Church there can be vehement disagreements over ideas but with good will toward what is really serious—the persons in which the ideas are embodied. We dispute on the street corner, but shake hands at Mass.

A divided Church? It can seem so, but perhaps thanks only to the attention given by the media to the few but noisy combatants. This is nothing new: even during his lifetime, Escrivá was often a "sign of contradiction" in the Church. Loved, revered, or at least respected by many, he was opposed by others; this happens to every strong personality, and is a kind of constant in the history of Christianity, beginning with Jesus.

Furthermore, the request to open the process of beatification of *El Padre* was presented to the Pope by one-third of the world's bishops. To be precise, 69 cardinals, 241 archbishops, and 987 bishops signed and sent their petitions (*supplicia*) to Rome. With these were more than fifty superior generals of the Church's more prestigious Orders and Congregations of Religious. Something else unusual was the number (about 80,000) of reports of "favors," "graces," and "prodigies" obtained through the intercession of Monsignor Escrivá in the years after his death: an amount unprecedented in the annals of the Church.

Equipped with its own support of both hierarchy and people, Opus Dei was able to win the "Battle for St. Peter's Plaza"—in "only" seventeen years, of which fewer than seven were actually required for the process. A long time for the world, but quite short for the Church, even though it is not a record. In reply to the criticisms about the relatively short time period, the Prelature's Office of Postulation replied that other causes, such as that of Francis Cabrini, the saint of immigrants to America, were just as fast, and that these were furthermore done in accordance with preconciliar norms, which exacted twice the requirements compared to the post-Vatican II norms of the Congregation for the Causes of the Saints.

The years of the Escrivá process were filled with something like 980 sessions of canonical tribunals, in which 265 standard questions were posed to each of ninety-two witnesses who had personally known the founder of the Work (there were additional questions as well, depending on the nature of the case). Practically every hour of every day of the candidate's life was carefully inspected to verify the complete fidelity of his life and of his thought to the Gospel and the Church.

For an even greater guarantee of accuracy, the "other side" was also heard: eleven ex-members, both numeraries and supernumeraries who had left the Work, and not always peacefully, were battered by questions. Then, too, the voice of the "neutrals": one-half of all the witnesses were purposely chosen from among the ranks of men and women who were not members of the organization.

The Work marches on. Don Flavio Capucci was the priest of the Work who, as postulator, coordinated the complex operation that lasted years and led up to the event in the Piazza San Pietro. A year after the beatification, in June 1993, he could report that there were "more than seven thousand stories, all signed and verified, of graces received, throughout the world, at the intercession of Blessed Escrivá."

Since a second miracle is required to reach "canonization," or to enter his name on the Canon or official list of saints, Don Capucci stated that his Office of Postulation was working to confirm the reports. A canonical process thus continues, the outcome of which is doubted by few. To confirm the popular movement that surrounds Escrivá, it was further reported that over a million persons, on all continents, attended the Masses when the liturgical feast of the new blessed was celebrated for the first time.

Don Capucci closed his remarks with a statement quoted from an article in a Spanish newspaper: "The controversy over the beatification has crashed like an outdated airplane against the old and solid walls of St. Peter's."

*Opus Dei itself never supported General Francisco Franco's regime (1939–1975), and the Prelature never gets involved in politics—not in Spain or anywhere else. Allow the facts to speak for themselves.

The temporal affairs of each member—whether in politics, economics, choice of work, or anything else—is a personal choice which he or she makes

freely and on his or her own responsibility in accordance with Christian principles. A few members of Opus Dei were involved in the regime, but, given the
lay nature of Opus Dei and its popularity among professionals, it would be surprising if some members of Opus Dei had not served in the Spanish government. And the facts actually indicate that fewer members of Opus Dei
participated in Franco's government than the media would have us believe. Of
the 116 ministers named by Franco for the 11 different cabinets that existed
from 1939 to 1975, only 8 were members of Opus Dei. There were no members of Opus Dei in the Spanish government until 1957; there were none in the
final cabinet. Of the 8 who did serve under Franco, 1 died 3 months after his
appointment, and another 4 were in office for only 1 term. At no time did
members come close to representing a majority in any cabinet. The myth of an
Opus Dei dominated Franco government is just that—a myth.

Moreover, several known members of Opus Dei were opposed to the regime.
Rafael Calvo Serer, editor of the daily *Madrid*, was hounded into exile for his
criticism of Franco, who closed the publication. Working underground, Calvo
Serer helped to bring democracy to Spain. Antonio Fontan was likewise a journalist who advocated free elections and trade unions. He too was persecuted,
but after Franco's death he returned as president of the Senate in 1977 to help
draft Spain's new democratic constitution.

Also significant is that the Falange, the political arm of the Franco regime,
conducted several smear campaigns in the press against Opus Dei over the
years. The Falangists were opposed to the liberal tendencies of the so-called
technocrats—some of whom were members of Opus Dei, including Alberto
Ullastres and Mariano Navarro Rubio—who wanted to modernize the economy and introduce cultural freedoms.

Beyond the specific numbers, however, the key to understanding the subject
is the freedom of lay Catholics working in temporal affairs. As Blessed
Josémaría expressed it: "Respect for its members' liberty is an essential condition of Opus Dei's very existence.... Opus Dei has never intervened in politics
and, with God's help, it never will; but if it were to, I would be its number one
enemy."

WS

CHAPTER THREE

MANY CULTS, ONE PRELATURE

✝

ATTACKED ON THE "OUTSIDE" by constant and repetitive public denunciations, and attempts to interfere, including parliamentary investigation; attacked on the "inside" by Catholics who condemn its evangelical radicalism as "pre-Conciliar integrism" and its solid fidelity to the papal Magisterium as a "desire for restoration," the Work is also under fire—in all the West, but especially in the United States—from anticult movements.

This aspect of the struggle that swirls around the first Prelature of the Church is little known, even to Catholics. But the question ought to be studied to make clear the importance of the issue. The most accurate terms and information come from the Italian writer Massimo Introvigne, one of the best informed on the prolific growth of "new religions" at the international level. And, as usual, the truth turns out to be the exact opposite of what the "experts"—

31

the sociologists, the futurologists, and even the theologians and specialists in various fields of religious studies, including many priests and bishops—have predicted. Remember, the best definition of an "expert" is: "A person, whose principal job is to explain, from time to time and for pay, why he and his colleagues have made totally erroneous predictions."

In the present case, during the fifties and sixties and beyond, these specialists theorized about such things as "the total eclipse of the sacred in industrial civilization"; they assured us that the future would be "secularized"; they swore, in fact, that there would be no place in the technological and postmodern culture for the religious dimension.

Among the thousands, one expert, Rudolf Bultmann, naively entranced with progress, proclaimed the "demythologization" of the Gospel; that is, he purged anything that did not suit the science and reason of the late nineteenth century. Even now, in outdated clerical think tanks, some people take seriously Bultmann's caricature, his entirely theoretical "modern man."

And naturally, the opposite of his prophecy has come to pass. In the East, the massive effort to eradicate all faith in the transcendent from the heart of man and to convert him to atheistic materialism has not only failed but also has been spurned precisely because people do not want to renounce religion; flying in the face of all theory, they have made religion a social and political power.

The beginning of the end of the Marxist empire has an exact date—August 1980. It was then that the Polish workers of Gdansk barricaded themselves in the dockyards and began the first strike, in any communist country and for so many decades, that the Marxist regime did not have the courage to suppress violently. The workers placed two pictures on the railings—pictures that shocked the progressivists of the West who watched it all on television: an icon of the Madonna of Czestochowa and a drawing of "their" Pope, elected two years earlier, who had visited Poland the preceding summer. Those shots of the entrances to the barricades protected by the Madonna and the Pope, and opened only to the cardinal primate or some bishop, to thunderous applause; those images of the workers standing in line, waiting to make their confessions to priests dressed in cassocks and purple stoles, seated on stools in the courtyards; all this suddenly splintered the structures of thinking that had seemed solid as granite; it signaled the end of the ideological myths of modernity.

In the West, the predicted secularization has given way to an unprecedented explosion of sects, churches, esoteric groups, oriental cults, each with an impressively growing, often fanatical following. And every so often there emerge mass murders, ritual homicides, sexual or financial scandals. It gives added confirmation to G.K. Chesterton's words: "The catastrophe of the man of today is not that he believes in nothing. The catastrophe is that he believes in everything."

Jehovah's Witnesses, Mormons, Hare Krishna, Scientology, *Bambini di Dio,* New Age, Moonies: these are well-known realities with crowds of followers in Italy as well as elsewhere. And, as a result, there has been an attempt to include Opus Dei in the explosion of new religiosity. It has produced not only fervent disciples, but intransigent, if not fanatical, adversaries.

Let's listen to what Massimo Introvigne has to say. The quotation will be long, but it is worth the space because these sects are affecting a growing number of people. In the West it seems that almost everyone has—or will soon have—a relative or friend involved in some way with the mystical explosion that ushered in the twenty-first century, the century of "complete secularization."

So, on to our "expert":

> In the face of the proliferation of the new religions, which at times have frankly controversial aspects, certain opposed phenomena have arisen, which may

be referred to as an "anticult" movement. This has itself become the object of significant sociological and psychological analyses, and such analyses have clarified how the "anticult" movements, which are opposed to the "new religions," define some of these latter as "cults destructive of the personality," and insist on an hypothesis of "brainwashing," requesting repressive measures on the part of the state. This movement is a reality substantially different from the groups that oppose the new religions from the standpoint of an "official" or "historical" or "mainstream" religion.

While the protest against the "cults" can give the impression of unity, in reality it is not so, and the attentive observer cannot help but notice the interweaving of two diverse movements, originating from opposite quarters, with opposing interests, and whose contradictions sometimes dramatically collide.

On the one side, there is the traditional aversion to the new religions that comes from the churches and the traditional communities, which formulate a negative judgment of a primarily *doctrinal* nature. This judgment presupposes that there exists a truth, even in the field of religion, which man can attain in some degree, albeit with difficulty. There are criteria of truth and value, on the basis of which the new religions can be studied and subject to some kind of evaluation.

To this critique of religious provenance, however, there is opposed—more often than allied with—the "anticult" movement, the origins of which are normally to be found outside of religious circles. It takes its cue from the social alarm generated by the new religions to propose a critique of *all* "strong" religious experiences, whether these come from minority or majority religions. While the so-called "religious" critique of the new religions places emphasis on the objectionable aspects of the "cults" in the name of truth and values, the "anticult" movement, on the contrary, considers anyone to be in a "cult" who does not accept relativism, and who persists in believing that there exists truth, even in religious matters.

From this Introvigne draws the following conclusions:

It is a polemic whose ideological motivations are easily identifiable, and which slide easily from a critique of the "cults" into a critique of religion in gene-ral. In the official bulletin of one of the principal European associations of the "anticult" movement, the French ADFI (Association for the Defense of the Family and the Individual), Alain Woodrow, one of the leaders of the movement, wrote recently that "*a priori,* there is no reason to show any more indulgence to the churches than the cults...." "Even though," Woodrow adds, "after the last Council of the Catholic Church, we must realize that the climate has changed a great deal" and that "the secta-rian spirit of the Counter-Reformation is finally dead."

In particular, Woodrow is delighted that "fasting and other forms of asceticism have practically disappeared, and the regulation within seminaries and religious houses has become much more humane after the Council." Under these conditions, he can add that the Catholic Church is not (or rather, is *no longer*) a "cult";

but the question arises, how would the movement judge realities—which peacefully exist within the churches and majority communities—where "fasting and other forms of asceticism" have not in fact disappeared, together with "catechisms learned from memory" in the "spirit of the Counter-Reformation," and the idea of being part of the "one true Church"? It is a matter of absolutely familiar and traditional critiques, within a certain ideological, laicist ambiance, in confrontation with the Catholic Church and other Christian religious experiences. By making this the principal criterion for criticizing "cults," there is a risk of rendering unintelligible the very categories of "cult" and "new religions" (in so far as they are distinct from traditional religion) and a risk of reducing the argument to a general attack on religion.

Introvigne continues:

One important figure of the anticultic "lay" movement wrote that "between churches and cults there is a difference only of degree and amount of dosage," and finally that "the line of demarcation between *conversion* and *brainwashing* is very difficult to trace."

And here we arrive, at last, at the point of interest:

From this point of view, while the anticult movement directs its attacks against realities like Opus Dei, which evidently participate fully in the Catholic world, it is possible to expect that in the future (once the equivocations and ingenuousness have been put aside) there will be a growing division between the religious critique (in Italy, above all the Catholic one) of the new religions, conducted on a basis of doctrinal criteria or truth and values (and generally diffident about any interventions on the part of the state in matters of religion) and the attack, from a "laicist" milieu, upon "cults" and "cultism," the point of departure of which is precisely the refutation of the possible existence of every religious truth, "old" or "new"; and this latter would be accompanied by a denunciation (with the intention of obtaining legislative repression) of every "strong" religious experience, whether this experience takes place in a "traditional" or "alternative" context.

So writes Massimo Introvigne in *Cristianita,* May 1994.

Within this lucid general framework, our Work would appear to be one among many. In fact, the "anticult" movements have made it a prime target for years, as Introvigne assured me in a personal interview. "There is always some virulent article in their journals or reviews, usually concluding in a demand that the public authorities make Opus Dei illegal. One of their most effective weapons is the scandal about the use of the *cilice,* as personally practiced by Blessed Escrivá and recommended to his followers (but under precise conditions and limitations). These anticults seem obsessed with the *cilice,* as if it were not the free, voluntary choice of free adult persons, and as if it were imposed upon them" (more on this controversial asceticism, including the *cilice* and the *flagellum,* in later chapters).

At an international convention titled "Totalitarian Groups and Cultism" convened at Barcelona in April 1993, a Spanish sociologist named Alberto Moncada (an "ex," I was told), after a violent denunciation of Opus Dei, expressed the hope that "the organization would be classified as one of the cults that are dangerous for children." A strange demand, seeing that the Work does not accept anybody under eighteen, and even then, only provisionally. At any rate, Professor Moncada was pleased to announce the establishment at Pittsfield, Massachusetts, of a network dedicated solely to combating Opus Dei around the world.

According to Massimo Introvigne, "In reality what disturbs some people, and often scandalizes them, about Opus Dei, is the process of conversion that many in it are living, by taking the evangelical demands 'too seriously' for the tastes of those (perhaps in the Church itself) who would like to reduce the Christian life to an ethics, a morality, a civic education, or a kind of socio-political motivation acceptable to everyone."

In any event, one of the motives for combating the cults (as Opus Dei is thought to be) is the financial shenanigans supposedly practiced by all leaders of religious groups. This is particularly surprising because these anticult movements, so virtuous in appearance, seem to have become a lucrative business. What generally occurs is that the "victim of the cult" is apprehended, thrown into a van, taken to a remote house or motel room, and "deprogrammed." In Spain alone, some dozens of young people aspiring to membership in Opus Dei have been victims of these violent "cures."

The purpose of the deprogramming is to counteract the "brainwashing" which has allegedly been perpetrated by the cult. And the cost of the process, often unsuccessful, comes to about $50,000 for the parents or friends who have requested the intervention of the deprogrammers.

According to many students of this disturbing phenomenon, the insistence on including Opus Dei as a dangerous cult that needs forcible deprogramming is the result of a deliberate strategy. In the United States, especially, the anticult movements flourish in environments of radical anti-Catholicism.

Not, of course, against the Church in its attenuated form in some countries. No: the battle is clearly with the Church of the

Pope, a "harsh" Pope who reacts against the dominant mentality and remembers the demands of a Gospel which necessarily divide and provoke opposition. The enemy appears to be a Church that instead of seeking approval, speaks of the unsettling, and for many today, *intolerable* words of the Gospel: "Do you think I have come to bring peace upon the earth? No, I say, it is for division...." (Lk. 12, 51).

Thus the people who are against Opus Dei are actually aiming higher—the Vatican itself is their target. Because of its faithfulness to the papacy, Opus Dei is seen as the modern equivalent of the once-feared Jesuits or as a new army of Knights Templar.

Here, too, is a source of support for the anticult movements, a support sometimes hidden, sometimes known to certain Catholic adversaries of the Work. These Catholics are preoccupied with one thing—the Work believes "too much," it takes "too seriously" the paradoxical and radical message of the Gospel.

Thus the people who are against Opus Dei are actually aiming higher— the Vatican itself is their target.

As for the media, just glance at the newspapers of the world and it becomes clear that the English-language press devotes only meager—and then scornful—attention to Catholic matters: at best, the Church is picturesque folklore, material for postcards, a lullaby for children.

This same press has been propelled by the beatification of Monsignor Escrivá to launch a front-page campaign, lasting for weeks, of venomous articles directed against the Pope. It is possible to document the close connections between the newspapers (whose owners can be shown to be stubbornly, even fanatically, anti-Catholic), and the anticult movements, especially in the United States. They attempt to make readers believe that the Pope has sanctioned "the exaltation of a Spanish fanatic, the creature of a secret lobby, and the instigator of other fanatics"; in doing so, the Pope not only bares his true feelings toward "liberal" tolerance, but also covers with his authority a sham process of beatification, a process that was successful only because of money, or perhaps through blackmail by some hidden powers. Among other accusations, some charged that in exchange for the title of Blessed for its founder, the Work promised to rescue the Vatican Bank from its severe financial straits, created by the speculative maneuvers of an American Archbishop, the unlucky Paul Marcinkus. According to these critics, the Pope thus compromised his infallibility in beatifications and canonizations: the "Escrivá Scandal" and the "Opus Dei Operation" made the dogma itself lose credibility. If the campaign against Escrivá had been successful, it would have opened a notable fissure in the very doctrinal edifice of the Catholic Church. The ax was not merely striking the branches, but was laid at the very roots of the ecclesiastical tree.

But to the point: just what *is* Opus Dei? What is this institution that has stirred up such love and such hatred from the very beginning? How was it born? How did it grow? And how is this *sign of contradiction* organized?

It was "born" in 1928 (the citation marks will become clear after I have explained this "birth"), and since November 28, 1982, seven years after the death of the founder on June 26, 1975, the *Societas Sanctae Crucis et Operis Dei,* its official name, became and remains the only Personal Prelature of the Catholic Church.

And what is a Personal Prelature?

The most accurate answer is the official one—the definition found in the thick volume bound in red with gold lettering known as the *Annuario pontificio,* published by the Holy See's Secretariat of State.

This authoritative book states: "Personal Prelatures are jurisdictional structures not circumscribed by territorial perimeters, and having for their purpose the promotion of an adequate distribution of priests or the actualization of special pastoral initiatives or missions to diverse regions or social categories."

This institution, new in the history of the Church, which appears to have tried every possible canonical form over two thousand years, was foreseen by the Second Vatican Council and was more exactly defined by a *motu proprio* and other pontifical documents following the council. The *Annuario pontificio* resumes: "It is the duty of the Apostolic See, after having heard from the relevant episcopal Conferences, to erect the Personal Prelatures and to confirm their statutes. They are governed by a prelate, as by their own ordinary, who has the right to erect a national or international seminary, and to incardinate the graduates."

It concludes: "The possibility has been foreseen that lay persons can be dedicated to the apostolic works of the same Prelature by means of contracts with the Prelature. The canonical ordinance now in effect further provides that the statutes will define the relationships of the Prelature with the ordinaries of the place in whose particular churches the Prelature develops its own pastoral and missionary works, with the consent of the diocesan bishop."

The language of canon law. Necessary, though, and even indispensable: in matters having to do with the institutional ordering of the Church, every word has been weighed and sifted by decades, if not centuries, of study, debate, and above all, experience. In the ecclesiastical community, life always precedes law. The proverbial slowness of the Vatican is born from a refusal to heed illuminations and from an antipathy to the ideological schemes of intellectuals.

To return to the official definition of a Prelature:

More intelligible, perhaps, is the reply Bishop del Portillo once gave in an interview to the question, "What is a Personal Prelature, and what is the Personal Prelature of Opus Dei, in particular?" His answer: "It is a hierarchical structure of the Church which joins priests and lay people under the jurisdiction of a prelate, to bring about a specific apostolic goal among ordinary Christians who live in the midst of the world, by teaching them how to transform into prayer the work that is normal for each, through an encounter with God."

This can be made a little more intelligible by offering another definition, effective because of its brevity: "A Personal Prelature constitutes a juridically structured pastoral program of the Church."

You have just learned what it took Opus Dei fifty-four years to obtain—its "prelatical" status, which, as its directors say, fully realizes the aspirations of the organization and can be considered as the definitive point of arrival.

For over half a century the Work searched for a place within the canon law of the time, "shedding many tears," to use Escrivá's words, while it accepted what came from the Holy See as a lesser evil, provisionally and with reservations to "moor at a dock that was not its own in the harbor of the Church."

This last expression is also the founder's, who died before the Work could cast its anchor to the shore that it had so long desired. But he never doubted that it would be reached. In 1951, Escrivá wrote to his followers: "I do not know when the appropriate juridical solution will come. But even if I do not know the time, even if I think it will require a few years, I say again, I have no doubt it will come."

There was another heated squabble concerning this canonical path of Opus Dei. From studying this seemingly endless dossier, it boils down to this. On the one side are the people of Opus Dei who maintain that everything was clear from the beginning; Monsignor Escrivá "saw" precisely what he was supposed to create, and struggled to realize that vision. On the other side are those who say that the Work, like other Catholic institutions, proceeded through a series of approximations, seeking its canonical place on the basis of experience accumulated along the way.

This does not appear to me to be an irresolvable conflict.

For one thing, this explains one of the reasons for the Work's reputation of excessive discretion, or even secrecy. Without an institutional slot in the Church's canon law of the time, the Work was forced to accept the juridical status of "Secular Institute," which effectively made its members who wanted to remain completely lay seem to be disguised religious. Hence the Work did not tend to publish its regulations, the statutes given it by the Holy See.

But these canonical norms (the statutes) were not secret, as it has been and still is claimed: they could be freely consulted by anyone who wished to see them—and of course they were explicitly accepted by every member—even though there was always a certain reservation about a structure that was considered inadequate and temporary.

From this discretion, an indication of discomfort, terms like "secret laws" or "hidden, unspeakable statutes" sprang up. But once the goal of the Prelature was reached—the *Codex iuris particularis Operis Dei,* the specific norms which regulate the institution and the duties of its members—the document was published without any hesitation, and appears as an appendix in practically every book that deals with the subject, including those written by Opus Dei members.

At any event, the founder was dead by the time the Work attained its final mooring, and the role of the first prelate of the Society of the Holy Cross and of Opus Dei was assumed by Alvaro del Portillo, a man over sixty at the time but still in fine form. He had been a civil engineer, later received doctorates in Philosophy and Canon Law, and for over forty years had been the closest collaborator of Blessed Josémaría; the General Congress of the Work had voted him unanimously and without hesitation to be his successor. Del Portillo kept the Work going at its steady and irresistible pace, without any problems and in full continuity with what had preceded him. In other words, the crisis feared by many, and hoped for by others, which often occurs in the Church at the death of a charismatic leader who has given life to a new institution, did not happen in this case.

The choice of del Portillo as prelate was also approved by the Holy See, an approval given further confirmation by his consecration as bishop by John Paul II in St. Peter's in January 1991. Now, although a Personal Prelature, to put it sketchily but comprehensibly, is like a "diocese with a people, but no defined territory"—the territory of Opus Dei is the whole world, and its "people" are its members—and although the head of a diocese by definition is a bishop, it is possible for the prelate not to have episcopal dignity. Thus del Portillo's canonical status lacked nothing from 1982 to 1991 when he governed the first Prelature in the history of the Church. But his elevation to bishop, apart from being a sign of the Church's favor, gave him the power to consecrate the clergy incardinated in his own Prelature, and in this way he further augmented its prestige. It also caused his enemies to renew their suspicions and to accuse Opus Dei of being a kind of "parallel Church."

Opus Dei is like a "diocese with a people, but no defined territory."

But these accusations ignore, among other things, an undeniable fact: Opus Dei is not a group of consecrated "brothers" and "sisters," or a congregation or order, or an "Institute of Perfection" that is subject, according to the norms of Canon Law, to the Vatican Congregation for Religious. Since it is not governed by a superior but by a prelate, and is subject to the Congregation for Bishops, Opus Dei is part of the hierarchical structure of the Church. And thus it too is "the Church," and by the same canonical logic cannot be a "parallel Church."

In any event, dangers of this kind seem to be all the more improbable in virtue of the fact that the Work professes fidelity, according to the norms by which it is bound, to the Holy See and to the Pope in particular—a fact that causes distrust among those same people who suspect the Work of wanting to "go its own path" toward a "restoration."

Moreover, at the lower level, as it were, its own statutes do not permit the Work to set up Centers, or even initiate an apostolate, without the previous, explicit consent of the bishop of the region in question, and the Work must then periodically keep the bishop informed about its activity as it enters fully into the local church.

Therefore, the Prelature has to *ally itself* with the bishops and the local dioceses, not be a *substitute* for them. A collaborator, not an antagonist. That matters really are operating in this fashion is confirmed by something already mentioned: An unprecedented number of the world's bishops—more than a third—"implored" the Pope to approve the beatification of Monsignor Escrivá.

CHAPTER FOUR

INSIDE THE "WORK"

BEFORE I CONTINUE, LET me describe one of the stops I took in my tour inside the Work. Among other things, it gives me the chance to anticipate something I will return to later in more detail.

Both before and during my investigation, I read what there was to be read in the languages I know, beginning with those languages in which the official documents are written, occasionally Latin, but usually Spanish.

Above all, of course, I read and reflected on the book that is both "engine" and "carburetor" of the institution: *The Way (Camino)*, definitively edited in 1939 (the earliest version appeared five years earlier), and a kind of world record-holder in the publishing industry, with its millions of copies in dozens of languages, including Peruvian Quechua and Philippine Tagalog.

It has 999 short thoughts (three multiples of three, in honor of the Blessed Trinity), which address the reader informally and guide him or her to a classic Catholic spirituality. Eleven years after the death of the founder in 1986, another thousand thoughts were published under the name of *Furrow (Surco)*. A year later, one more collection, this time numbering 1,055, was published as *The Forge (Forja)*. Escrivá wrote other books as well (for example, one on the Rosary, over a million copies), but these three (especially *The Way*) contain the real flesh and blood of his thought, and consequently, of Opus Dei.

I studied all available published material (both pro and con) as well as files, mimeographs, and photocopied sheets. Not a single request was denied. I was supplied with everything I asked for from their mythical archives.

They arranged appointments with the people I wanted to meet—from a Naples policeman (a member of the Work) to the nearly inaccessible prelate himself. I spent about two hours with him, plying him with questions in his study at Rome.

I stayed for a considerable time in the EUR (Espozione Universale di Roma) district at the International University Residence in an assigned suite. This is a "corporate apostolic work" (a term explained later) where I shared meals and *tertulias* with the members who direct the operation and work as tutors for the students (in addition to their outside professional work). *Tertulia,* a Castilian word, means the brief gathering that follows lunch and dinner in every Center. It is a chance to relax in the living room and exchange comments, impressions, and friendly conversation.

This takes place in the company of guests as well in a normal family atmosphere; they explain that it is an essential characteristic of the Work. Opus Dei was born in the house of the young Don Josémaría Escrivá in a middle-class Madrid home of the twenties and thirties kept by his mother and sister. Here, too, was born the good taste previously mentioned, which characterizes the places where guests are received and live together. Poverty is lived—I saw it firsthand—but it was behind the lines, in the rooms of the members of the Work or in the places where only they usually go (not a cloister, which would be inconceivable for the lay spirit of the organization). "We ought to do penance for ourselves, and not impose it on others," Don Escrivá used to say, recommending a "smiling asceticism," that was the more meritorious the less it was displayed.

While at Rome I also visited a women's Center, and there too I asked questions of any and all, whether foreign members of the Work or the young guests, an overwhelming majority of whom were not members. This was also a university residence. Here, as in all the places where there are women of the Prelature, one particular detail caught my journalist eye: married women, the supernumeraries, and unmarried women, the numeraries, were all carefully dressed, quite different from nuns, and could not be distinguished from other women of similar social background.

I also passed an entire day at that great apostolic work, the ELIS Center built in 1965, which stands in the popular Tiburtine district, and which is one of the largest, most efficient, and renowned centers of professional formation in Rome, if not in all Italy. It includes residences for young workers and artisans, athletic centers (almost fifty thousand boys visit it every year, most of them nonmembers), guest rooms, and a library.

Nearby, the women's branch of the Prelature directs the professional hotel school. The reputation of the school is so high that 90 percent of the girls who graduate from it find work immediately, the other 10 percent a little later.

Among the subjects taught is the preparation of fine dishes (good to look at and good to eat) from simple ingredients. They also learn the art of transforming a modest house into an attractive home, making judicious use of upholstery, curtains, lamps, proper arrangement, and other little stratagems—everything rigorously economical and "do-it-yourself." Once again, the idea is to do it well, to be sparing in everything but labor and ingenuity.

The ELIS Center was built on land and with funds made available by John XXIII (who used the money collected from the whole world for the eightieth birthday of Pius XII), inaugurated by Paul VI, and visited by John Paul II. Opus Dei is proud of this papal sponsorship since it confirms that they have been supported by a variety of Popes. The ELIS Center forms thousands of young men and women for the professions and has done for the Roman economy something analogous to what the Valdocco of Don Bosco did for Turin in the nineteenth century, with its trade and artisan schools.

The ELIS Center—Opus Dei's center in Rome for the training of professionals—was built on land and with funds made available by John XXIII, inaugurated by Paul VI, and visited by John Paul II—all instances of public papal sponsorship confirming the mission of Opus Dei.

The Center is completed by a church, which functions as a local parish, and is in the care of the priests of the Prelature.

I attended Sunday Mass in this church, where I saw good works of contemporary art, not easily found today, an abundance of flowers, a liturgy faithful to official norms, a choir of local youths perfectly conducted (and supported by a professional organist), and a group of concelebrating priests of various nations and ethnic groups.

A place and time—at least one hour a week—of beauty and royal dignity for the people of one of the most squalid and desolate suburbs of Rome. Participating in this Mass, I felt sure that this, too, could be social activism, and of a very relevant kind—to offer to each attendant the opportunity of participating in something quite different, even in external appearance, from the daily grind.

Continuing my tour of inspection, I visited professors and students at the Pontifical Atheneum of the Holy Cross. This was intended as the Roman bridgehead for the University of Navarre, but through some giant steps it is becoming a pontifical university like the Lateran or the celebrated Gregorian of the Jesuits. Numerary members of Opus Dei study at its schools of philosophy, theology, and canon law, as do seminarians and priests sent by bishops around the world who want solid doctrine. (A School of Church Communications was added in 1996.) It is a theological factory where those panzers Don Giussani mentioned are produced, where there is training in that soft but decisive method that characterizes those of Opus Dei.

Read the catalogue put out by the faculty, so strategic for the whole Church, the faculty of theology at this Atheneum planted here in the city of the Pope: "Our mission is to deepen and to expound Catholic doctrine... our intention is to form experts *in the science of the faith....*"

You may recall Benedetto Croce's ironic words about theology: "these words about things whose existence is unknown."... In Opus Dei, there is no hesitation about whether these things exist. The certainties the philosophers and scientists believe they have discovered have wound up as so many erudite curiosities, whereas at the Pontifical Atheneum they are more than ever convinced that "theology is a science and can, and ought, to be taught *scientifically.*" To give an idea of how things are done here, the entrance to the ancient and illustrious plaza of St. Apollinaire, the new site of the Atheneum, has a sign stating that diocesan priests must wear ankle-length cassocks or "clericals" when attending classes, and members of religious orders must wear their habits. The priests of Opus Dei never appear in anything other than priestly apparel. They are immediately recognizable as different, in the sense of providing a witness to another reality, a witness that begins with an external appearance that speaks openly of that further dimension.

As for the curriculum, the students there assured me that it provides a great deal, not just in terms of solid academics, but also concrete help with the way things are done at Rome, including tutorial assistance in addition to the lectures. And it demands the best, at least at the level of effort.

And once again, the seriousness of the enterprise has been rewarded: the numbers show the escalation familiar to Opus Dei. In 1984, when the Atheneum opened—it began quietly as an academic center, a mere branch of the University of Navarre—there were only forty students. In 1994, there were six hundred from fifty-five different nations, half from Europe, half from the other continents.

This Atheneum seems destined to become increasingly important in forming the governing class of the Church, even if the members in what they call "collective humility" will not say so. Here, Tradition with a capital T—in these postmodern times it is not clear how better to define it—is revealed as the most direct highway into the future. At the Roman Atheneum of the Holy Cross the pedagogical methods, the tools of learning and research, are the most *avant garde,* but what is taught there is in line with the strictest fidelity to the Magisterium. As I said before, the future may turn out to be something that represented the past to those obsessed with the new.

I met with the same strong mix of traditional content and modern methods, at once daring and pragmatic, but on a much larger and more complex scale, not at Rome but in another stage of my journey, the ancient capital of the Kingdom of Navarre. For most, the city of Pamplona is not known for the wound received there in 1521 by the *hidalgo* Ignatius of Loyola as he defended the city from the besieging French, and even less for the brief episcopacy of the unedifying Caesare Borgia, the son of Pope Alexander VI, that cruel and brilliant adventurer who ignited the illusions of Machiavelli. For most, Pamplona is bound up not with religious history, but rather with Hemingway's bullfights, the thunderous images of the bulls running freely through the streets of the city, pursuing mobs of young men seeking death-defying thrills.

Spanish folklore is rich in values, symbolism, human meaning, and religious echoes. But Spanish folklore does not appear to have any place in the huge, 400-square kilometer campus, neatly trimmed with flowers, shrubs, and 30,000 trees. The modern buildings for the various departments or faculties of the university and the many *colegios mayores* (university residences) are dominated by the administrative building, modern as well, but with towers, escutcheons, tympani, and staircases that recall something of the glory of Catholic imperial Spain. It speaks of a Spain conscious of a providential role in the world, and also in the Church: it is not by chance that the majority of the world's Catholics speak the language of Castile, which since Charles V, or debatably Philip II, became familiar in Heaven itself.

Founded in 1952, the university was long desired by Blessed Escrivá, who was its grand chancellor until his death in 1975. Above all, it has the merit of having broken the state monopoly imposed by Spanish secularism on all higher education in Spain: the Jacobin centralism that decreed that no degrees could be conferred except by a university controlled by the government in Madrid.

Today at Pamplona degrees are offered in law, medicine, literature, philosophy, pharmacy, natural sciences, canon law, information sciences, architecture, and languages. These subjects are studied in such a way and with such organization that a recent study by the European Community classified the University of Navarre as among the best, if not the best, of the continent. Here, too, the motto of Escriváis at work: "Whatever you do, do it well. Poorly done things cannot be offered to God."

My plane arrived at the small but modern airport at Pamplona. The university has changed the life of this city of under two hundred thousand inhabitants: almost half a million persons pass through here annually, on business connected in some way with the university. I was entrusted to the professional public relations staff.

Computer printouts provided me with all the numbers, charts, and diagrams I wanted. There were around fifteen thousand students there, about 10 percent of them from foreign countries all over the world. The number is considered large enough to offer adequate services, and for the present small enough to avoid crowding and to allow the personal approach sought after by Opus Dei from the start, not just here in its own university.

Thus in the colleges of the university, in the Centers of formation, or in apostolic activities, people are divided into groups not much larger than ten each, in contrast to the mass community and the collective even in the years of its popularity. Each is personally attended to in his or her religious, moral, cultural, and professional formation. It says no to anonymity, and yes to the individual as a unique piece in God's design. This is of primary importance in the Work's structure, an anomaly in a century known for its collectivist utopias.

Opus Dei's integral formation says no to anonymity and yes to the individual as a unique piece in God's design.

I believe that Escrivá, like the famous French convert Andre Frossard, was convinced that "the Christian God only knows how to count to one," and that He is a God Who is not interested in "humanity" but in concrete men and women, each with a name; a God Who does not recognize classes, parties, or races but only individuals, equal in their rights and obligations, at once unrepeatable, inimitable, and nontransferable.

But to continue. In regard to study, too, the university wants above all to be person-centered. There are 1,900 professors— one for each ten students—and an even larger number of young people are engaged in tutoring; 4,000 employees; 18,000 applications for admission every year for the 2,000 available places; and 40,000 licentiate degrees have been awarded over the past forty years.

Furthermore, in Barcelona, the economic capital of Spain, the *Instituto de estudios superiores de la empresa* (IESE), founded in 1958, has become one of the most prestigious centers in the Western world for postgraduate business training, producing MBAs of international prestige. In 1993, it had 117 teachers of fifteen nationalities and only 420 highly select graduates from fifty-eight countries, who took twenty months of intensive training for posts of executive responsibility. Here too, in the heart of modernity, management lives very well with the Mass and Rosary. The following statement to prospective students reveals the spirit of the institution: "The direction of business enterprises is a job entrusted to persons and is oriented to other persons. The instruction at IESE always emphasizes the human and ethical meaning, the conscience, in every business decision. The greatest professionalism must coexist with an unfailing spirit of service for the benefit of persons."

Perhaps an Italian journalist would suspect that all of this implies an elite, that here, too, the exclusivity of the Opus Dei is in evidence. But at this point a touch on the computer brings a colorful diagram to the screen: according to the statistics for the academic year 1992–93, a large part of the students (44 percent) came from families of small incomes, 40 percent from families of middle income, and only 16 percent from high-income families. In a typical year the university provides 350 million pesetas in *becas* (or grants), dispensations, and other kinds of aid. This includes the hospitality of the *colegios,* so that no one coming from a distant land has to make arrangements, or worse, give up study because of failure to find proper lodgings.

Nor does this present a facade of philanthropy with public money. Another screen states that the contribution of the

Spanish government amounted to 0.2 percent—zero point 2 percent. The University of Navarre, the only university in this peripheral part of the country, serves the whole nation but especially the rather poor regions where it was purposely located, and deeply rooted, so as not to give the impression of an "alien space colony"; 85 percent of its funding is by registration and tuition, 11 percent by assistance received by the Association of Friends (an association of alumni), and 2 percent from the subventions of various private and public entities at the local level.

Only half of the professors are members of Opus Dei—there are more members in chairs of state universities throughout Spain than in their own university in Pamplona. Moral and religious formation is offered as an option to the students.

The functional atmosphere of this institution is seen in another fact told me by the rector himself: in almost forty years, from 1952 to 1992, including the late sixties, no emergency repressive measures had to be taken. Over this period, the University of Navarre was closed a total of twelve days because of student agitation, a little more than one day every four years. The average for the state universities was over sixty days *per year*.

To sum up, a professor explained with disarming confidentiality what he felt was the secret of the stability and the seriousness at Pamplona in the years when universities throughout the world—Catholic included—were ravaged by the follies of the late sixties. "You know," he told me, "we prayed more than ever to the Holy Spirit, that He inspire these poor young people—who could so easily fallen prey like their contemporaries to the bad teachers of the day—to do their best."

This goes far to explain the extraordinary (in the etymological sense of the word) atmosphere of Opus Dei: up-to-date professional preparation and traditional devotion; computers and novenas to the Paraclete.

But on the emotional level, the real heart of the huge campus at Pamplona seemed to me to be located in the buildings of the university clinic. While eating at the cafeteria provided for doctors, patients, and guests, I noted at a nearby table no less than the king and queen of Spain. The father of Juan Carlos had come down with a serious illness, and it was decided that he should come here rather than any sophisticated private clinic or state hospital. This clinic is open to the king, as well as to anyone else.

I interviewed the smiling director of the General Clinic, a handsome numerary with a trim athletic physique, in a beautiful office that was fully computerized, overlooking the campus. I began by saying, "As I can see, you are a doctor...." "As you can see, I am not a doctor but an economist...." was his lightening reply.

In short, he was a manager for a hospital of 1,300 employees, three hundred of them medical doctors who gave up private practice to work in the clinic. There are 12,000 patients per year, in five hundred rooms, a large portion of which are single rooms that provide overnight stays for a parent or relative, and none larger than double rooms. There are 90,000 outpatient cases or consultations a year, a school for five hundred nurses, a hundred heart-transplants and more than five hundred kidney-transplants are performed, and testing in what is supposed to be one of the most difficult operations, the liver transplant.

Here there is no assistance from the state, not even the 0.2 percent received by the other departments. Yet the budget is always in the black, thanks to the payment for services rendered by the insurance companies and mutual-aid associations.

Further—and this, I found, is a constant of the apostolic activities of Opus Dei—economic assistance and offerings come not only from members of Opus Dei but also from friends who often are not Catholics or even Christians but who are convinced of the value to society of such an enterprise. Here as in all places where men and women of the organization are present, the Spanish saying holds, *cada palo aguante su vela,* "every ship with its own sail"—that is, every initiative has to find its own means of financing, following the principles of professionalism and not of dependency. This does not exclude charitable donations.

Unlike public hospitals, the clinic tries to offer personal attention, professionalism, care for big and small things alike, workers who feel they are collaborators and not mere employees, organization without bureaucratic oppression, openness to families and friends to overcome the isolation of the patients, an integral understanding of health care that does not look on the body as a machine to be repaired, but as an individual to be helped toward a complete healing, and on and on.

Economic offerings come not only from members of Opus Dei but also from friends who often are not Catholics or even Christians.

They have not attained all these things. But at least they are all *trying to, every day,* according to another frequently repeated dictum of the founder: "to begin and begin again" *(comenzar y recomenzar).*

But words are words, and deeds are deeds. And of the latter, some are more revealing than others. I reflected on this truth as I was led down the corridors, busy with personnel in spotless uniforms, and through the quiet, well-equipped rooms, the gleaming bathrooms. Perhaps even those who look with suspicion and hostility on the Catholic world will, when the moment arrives, wish to make their end in a place like this rather than a place where thrives a culture of rights, ideological manifestos, abstract idealism, and political promises.

Perhaps this is what one of the medical professors, a supernumerary, wanted to communicate to me when he spoke of his own department, the clinic, as well as the whole Universidad de Navarre. He said, "All of us here are trying to build a reality that will work as an example—within our limits, of course—but placing our good will and trust in the help of the God in Whom we believe. The Blessed

Escrivá said that he was nothing other than a sinner, but a sinner who loves Jesus Christ. We, too, would like to offer deeds, which speak much louder than words. Doesn't the Gospel say so? If a tree is good, you will know it from its fruits, which will be good. Only with the proper humility—a humility which is the *truth* about our condition as poor men, and always limited—would we like to have people ask 'Why?,' 'Why are they doing it?' 'Who, or what, inspires them to do this, without being forced?'"

Another example was described to me by one of the faculty deans as I dined with the general staff in the rector's dining hall, a modern room decorated in the severe style of old Spain with colorful heraldic shields. "This complex of energy, intelligence, activity, is also intended to be the most concrete demonstration of the harmony of the Catholic faith, professed in its integrity, with the most rigorous culture, a demonstration that the believer is not beset by a mutually exclusive alternative between the free and full acceptance of the Catholic faith and working at the highest possible levels of science, art, and technology."

This distinguished professor directed me to the *Ideario,* a kind of decalogue which everyone here, whether members of the Work or not, is required to honor. Its twenty points sketched the general coordinates of the commitment required of anyone who freely chooses to become a part, at any level, of this community of study and labor.

Listen to one of the most important points of this *Ideario,* the third: "In all its activities, the University of Navarre has for its guide a complete faithfulness to the Church's Magisterium. . . in the conviction that when authentic scientific research proceeds with the strictest methods and in conformity with moral norms, it *cannot* come into opposition with faith, since reason and faith have their origin in one and the same God, the fountain of all truth."

I must stop my tour at this point for reasons of space. But I want to make clear that the high peaks which I have pointed out, these flowers of Opus Dei, are not the *whole* Opus Dei. On the contrary, they may not even be its most important aspect.

The principal aim of the organization is to give a meaning, a direction, a content, to what is ordinary and personal: work of whatever kind, from the most humble to the most prestigious; daily life; and the seeming monotony, or mediocrity, of family life. With regard to the apostolate, it takes place every day through one's profession, in saying the "right thing" to one's neighbor—at home, in the office, in the factory.

Finally, Opus Dei is not these corporate apostolic works nor even the "owner" of them. Opus Dei accepts responsibility only for their doctrinal and spiritual orientation. According to the clear statement of the statutes, such works can *never* be industrial, economic, commercial, or even editorial activities, but are always and exclusively oriented toward education, assistance, and social welfare. But they are still not the Work. This is something that goes on in the spiritual life which each member, after joining, commits himself to cultivate in his own conscience, and which, by definition, escapes external observation.

To anticipate somewhat, it could be said that of all the many "secrets" Opus Dei is accused of, this is probably the first and foremost. But as with any truly religious reality, what is not seen is much more—and much more important—than what is seen.

CHAPTER FIVE

A FOUNDER WITHOUT
A FOUNDATION

UNTIL NOW, I HAVE spoken only of the present—a present in which Opus Dei is able to do its work for God and continue its daily expansion within the Church as a Prelature with eighty thousand members.

But how did it all start? Where did it come from? How did this kind of organization come into being with its center at Rome but a reach to all the world?

One of the bigger surprises awaiting someone who wants to understand what Opus Dei is, is to learn that according to those involved in it, nobody founded it, in the proper sense of the word, nor did anybody dream it up.

It was already there, thought and willed *ab aeterno* by God Himself. In His inscrutable will, He chose as an instrument an obscure, twenty-six-year-old Spanish priest who would make this celestial idea concrete by putting at God's disposal his efforts, sacrifices, prayers, and intelligence. This total placing of himself at God's disposal began at an exact date: the morning of October 2, 1928.

Here we need to explain something to those who are not cognizant of Christian and especially Catholic logic, in order if not to accept, at least to *understand* the aspirations of this Work. And that is: the God of the Bible does not want to act alone; He needs human beings to realize His will in the world.

All Scripture—both the Old and New Testaments—is nothing other than a "history of salvation" which the Creator proposes and realizes not *without,* but *with* His creatures. He is of course completely capable of acting on His own, with a metaphorical snap of His omnipotent fingers. But instead, He chose to work first with the herdsman Abraham to bring His revelation, at the beginning, to the people of Israel; and, second with the fisherman Peter so that Peter could be the rock *(petros)* on which He would build His Church, the locus of unity for those called to be the New Israel, no longer limited to one people but extended to all.

The story of the saints is nothing other than the story of those who agreed to be *collaborators* with God, even more than His *instruments,* as countless Protestant denominations believe. The saints are those who said yes to the ultimate degree to a mysterious and gratuitous offer of partnership. And it is because of this that the Catholic Church offers these saints as an example to all the faithful; for each of them is called—each according to his own ability and personal situation—to work with God, Who calls him or her to be associated with Him in His plan for the world.

And thus the Catholic personal pronoun is not the "I" of God or of man, but the "we" of God and man together—not because of human merit, of course, but because of the free and inscrutable divine strategy.

In short, God could have worked by Himself, but He chose not to. It is up to the believer to discern His plan and to collaborate in it, accepting its consequences with both toil and joy, as the Church teaches.

To be sure, upon this mysterious plane, some rather huge peaks emerge since this collaboration, while proposed to all, consists for some in getting others involved in pointing the way for the many.

This has been the case particularly with regard to the founders and foundresses of orders, congregations, institutes, companies, and religious communities that have distinguished Catholic Christianity from its origins.

In my library, I have, close to hand, works of ready reference, such as the *DIP, The Dictionary of Institutes of Perfection,* a vast work that lists and describes all the manifestations of religious life that have existed in some organized mode in the history of the Church. Eight huge volumes in an encyclopedic format, each one over a thousand pages long, have consumed twenty years of labor; at present it is only at the letter "s". But the editors have stated that once they have reached the end of "z", they will have to add more volumes in order to include the institutes of perfection that have arisen in the meantime. Such are the ramifications of Noah's ark, or the exuberant and unfathomable wilderness called the Church.

A decision to take the faith seriously, to take it to the utmost, has been organized (and will continue to be as the Catholic adventure continues) in each of these communities, and their origin has always depended on God's offer, illumination, and assistance.

The collaboration of a person called to the task usually begins with the discovery of a current need in society or the Church. These circumstances call on the intervention of charity, based on faith, hope, good will, and the energy and effort of believers. And whoever becomes conscious of this need rolls up his sleeves and calls on other men and women of good will to collaborate in a beneficial, spiritual project.

Thus we see the foundations dedicated to the young and the old, the poor and the sick, the ignorant and the workers; accord-

ing to the needs which emerge at each moment, and which each
Christian (especially those who are called as clearly as they are
mysteriously) knows must be attended to, for the love of God and
neighbor.

Inspired and guided by the Most High, these founders or
foundresses, according to the need, elaborate a certain plan, or
carry out certain projects, and they organize in order to make these
plans a reality, trusting more in the help of God than in their own
strength, although they do not spare themselves but give everything they have. "Useless servants," according to the paradox of the
Gospel, and yet at the same time indispensable to the Almighty,
who wants to make use of their weakness; they are necessary for a
Heaven that wants to make a joint venture with earth.

But to return to our topic. According to the understanding of
Don Josémaría Escrivá and to those who have followed him, this
did *not* happen with Opus Dei—not at least in regard to a plan,
project, or foundation. "I am a founder without a foundation," he
would often say. And this was not merely the humility of a saint
speaking. "I did not want to be a founder of anything, and even
less so of something that would be called Opus Dei."

But in the surprising outcome probably lies the magnetism of
the adventure. To use Escrivá's words again: "It was not begun as
a result of my studies, or research, or because I realized that there
were certain problems that needed to be resolved at the time in
the Church in Spain, or even in the universal Church. No, I didn't
have any plan or project."

What really happened, according to the members of Opus Dei,
is this. In 1928 the young Don Escrivá had been a priest for three
years. To complete his studies in canon law, he moved to Madrid
with the permission of his ordinary, the archbishop of Zaragosa,
the historic capital of Aragon. He was born in Barbastro, a little
town of seven thousand inhabitants, within view of the Pyrenees,
roughly opposite Lourdes.

After his first assignment to some rural parishes, the newly ordained priest worked in the capital where, to support his studies and to help his widowed mother and older sister, he gave private lessons and accepted the position of chaplain at the Patronato de Enfermos, a charitable hospice founded by the women of Madrid.

Here, among the sick, he demonstrated his desire to take his priesthood seriously, dedicating himself completely to the works of catechesis, administrating the sacraments, and helping not only the patients at the Patronato but also the poor folk living in the barrios around Madrid.

He was only a young priest, one of the many in Spain just a few years prior to one of the bloodiest of modern civil wars. Not mere anticlericalism, but only hatred of religion itself, can explain the many excesses of the left-wing extremists—the anarchists, socialists, communists, and radicals. This included firing squads deployed against the statues of the saints in the plazas and obscene abuses of consecrated hosts.

To cite the objective assessment of an impartial historian: "The religious persecution which took place in Spain, especially during the first part of the war, had no precedent in any page of European history, unless we turn back to the first two centuries of the history of the Church. The mere fact of being a believer was enough to get one executed."

Two years before the full outbreak of the war in 1936, the blood was already flowing. In *one week alone* in 1934 in the Asturian prelude to the great tragedy, twelve priests, seven seminarians, and eighteen religious were massacred, and fifty-eight churches were burned to the ground.

When the civil war erupted in full force in July 1936, the bloodshed seeped through all the provinces under the control of the left-wing government in the most atrocious ways. These included crucifixion, being doused with gasoline and burned alive, being suffocated by having crucifixes jammed down the throat, and the mass rape and murder of nuns. These methods accounted for the death of 4,184 diocesan priests, 2,365 brothers, 283 monks, 13 bishops, and unknown thousands of other Catholics. At Barbastro itself, the native city of Don Escrivá, 88 percent of the clergy were massacred. Not even the dead were safe. Instances of necrophilia stun the sensibilities.

But back to 1928. The young Jose María's priesthood (later, out of devotion to Joseph and Mary, he united the two names into one) could not be ascribed to the Spanish tendency to have at least one priest or religious brother or sister; it was a choice made with conviction, apparently dating back to his sixteenth year. And it took place in an extraordinary way.

The story is recounted by one of Don Escrivá's more recent and best biographers, the German Peter Berglar: "One particularly cold morning between Christmas 1917, and the Feast of the Epiphany 1918, he noticed, in some freshly fallen snow, the prints of a Carmelite's bare feet. The sight of these footprints of a humble follower of Christ strongly moved the young man and set his heart on fire. Bare footprints in the snow... were not something that could be comprehended with one's natural reason or within a utilitarian framework. 'Prudent' people call certain things 'madness'.... And so, impressed by that discovery, his vocation to the priesthood which until that moment had remained hidden, began to be revealed...."

But what was he to do? How was he to express his religious zeal? As a parish priest? A professor? Chaplain? Canon lawyer?

Working and praying, he waited for God to enlighten him, looking for direction in the ordinary events and encounters of life by which Providence normally speaks rather than in some mystical experience.

The young man was both devout and serene: he prayed fervently, but at the same time was down-to-earth, the opposite of a visionary or of someone "who hears voices." In truth, before he chose the seminary he had been attracted to technical studies—

architecture and engineering—a passion he would put into practice when it came to building the headquarters of the Work in
Rome, or planning the huge Marian sanctuary at Torreciudad near
Barbastro. Another talent was acknowledged when he was only
twenty years old and was named internal inspector of the diocesan
seminary by the archbishop of Zaragosa, who spotted the young
priest's gifts of organization and leadership. All in all, he was an
unusually mature and gifted person.

Thus the day of October 2, 1928, dawned in an atmosphere free
of mystical agitation. The date is now celebrated the world over
by the members of Opus Dei, not so much as the anniversary of a
foundation or revelation of a divine project, but as an "instrument
of sanctification" issuing from the unfathomable depths of eternity and destined to last as long as the Church—until the end of
time when faith waits for the victorious and glorious return of
Christ.

The Work has no doubts about its duration, because the
Blessed Josémaría affirmed many times over that the presence and
expansion of the Work would continue "as long as there are
people on the earth.... However much the technological forms of
production change, men will always have work to offer up to God,
to sanctify"—in effect, the aim of the organization. He also said,
"We are not an organization that arose from the particular circumstances of a distinct era." And finally, "Opus Dei will always
keep its *raison d'etre.*"

What then happened on that fateful day? It was best
expressed by the postulator of the cause, since his words were
carefully weighed and carry a kind of official status, having been
authenticated by the Church in its Decree of Beatification pro-
mulgated by the Pope sixty-four years after the event: "On the
Second of October, 1928, the Servant of God Don Josémaría was
participating in a retreat at the home of the Missionary Fathers
of St. Vincent de Paul, located in Madrid in the *Calle Garcia de*

Paredes. While reflecting in his room, God saw fit to illuminate him: he *saw* Opus Dei, as God wanted it, and as it would have to be, over the course of centuries."

Peter Berlgar, his German biographer, adds: "Escrivá always insisted that Opus Dei was not his own invention, that it was not the consequence of a series of speculations, analyses, discussions, or experiments, and that it was not the result of good and pious intentions. He clearly implied that the actual founder was God himself and that the commission of the task to a young priest was a supernatural act, a unique grace."

This grace was frightening. The young priest said afterward that he received it *de mala gana* ("reluctantly") because "I didn't want to be a founder of anything."

But wanting nevertheless to obey God and His commission which had been so suddenly placed on his shoulders, he sought a way out: he began to look for something in the Church that would correspond with what he had "seen," and to associate with it and, as he wrote, "to become the lowliest member of it, and serve it." But this came to nothing, for the thing did not yet exist: it was he who had been designated to bring the divine will to actuality. When he looked around in that autumn of 1928, he realized that he "was twenty-six years old and had nothing besides the grace of God and a sense of humor."

He would have particular need of a sense of humor, for sixteen months later he received another surprise. On February 1, 1930, he wrote to a few friends, "This Work, which I have been asked to devote my life to build, will only be for men; it will never have women, even in jest." But on February 14 of that same year, while celebrating Mass in the small private oratory of the old marquesa of Onteiro, he *saw* Opus Dei again, in the same mysterious way, and realized that it was to be composed of men *and* women.

Here was one more problem, and not a small one. To begin with, it was difficult for a twenty-eight-year-old priest in the

Spain and Church of the thirties to recruit women. Then there were the problems of organization: a formula would have to be fashioned to ensure unity and separation at the same time. It was resolved by Don Josémaría as follows: "Opus Dei consists of two different sections, completely separate, like two distinct works, one masculine and one feminine, without any interference of government, economic administration, apostolate, or activities." Or more succinctly: "In the Work, the two branches are like two donkeys pulling the same cart in the same direction."

The image of the burro, the patient donkey who turns the millstone or the waterwheel at the well, was one of his favorites, and he often used it as an illustration for his sons, or male followers; in the same way, he compared his daughters to ducks who know how to swim as soon as they get in the water. Hence little figurines of donkeys or ducks are often seen in the Centers. (These, incidentally, are considered by some, like the *Economist* cited above, as "hidden signs of recognition," akin to the geometric signs and T-square of the Masons.)

The overwhelming majority of Opus Dei members are married persons.

The men's and women's sections, then, are not two divergent forces, but two energies that work together. They are united in the person of the prelate.

The overwhelming majority of Opus Dei members are married persons, and for them the man-woman relationship occurs in the context of what is required of a serious Christian family. The numeraries and associates, on the other hand, are dedicated to celibacy. The numbers of men and women are practically equal—38,500 female and 38,000 male members, according to 1993 statistics. (There are also 1,500 priests.)

The severity of the norms of the organization which makes for collaboration without intermingling, beyond what is strictly regulated, has given rise to smirks even in clerical circles. For some, it is "outdated bigotry"; for others, it is "prudent"and "realistic," needed to foster chastity in the present day.

But also keep in mind Don Escrivá's deep respect for matrimony, which he termed "a true vocation, a great sign of the Christian faith."

But back to his discovery during Mass with the old marquesa and the vision of "the other half of Heaven" which added so much to the young priest's burden. It was in actuality so heavy that he later said, "The foundation of Opus Dei took place *without me.*"

The story began on October 2—on that day the liturgy honors the Holy Guardian Angels, of which the Old and New Testaments are filled, and it came to have an important place in the spirituality of Opus Dei. And then came February 14, 1930. Together they were the story of a gardener who has been entrusted with a seed and who dedicates all his care, all his time, all his energies—his whole life–to the growth of the plant.

Knowing how this happened, we outsiders can better understand why his followers insist on calling him their father. For this priest and this organization are indivisible: Escrivá *is* Opus Dei in the same sense as the gardener and the plant that have been entrusted to him form a single unity.

So it happened that the life of this priest was apparently without great events as measured by eternal standards. It is the story–largely interior, and thus inaccessible—of a man's endeavor to be transformed into an instrument ever more malleable, teachable, and energetic in order to create and accept a project, a cross, that was conceived in Heaven and placed on his shoulders. But as he advised his followers: "Isn't it true that, when you stop being afraid of the cross–of what people call "a cross"—when you apply your will to accepting the Divine Will, you are happy and all your preoccupations, all your physical and moral sufferings, pass away?"

To find out about Opus Dei in an objective manner, to learn about its spirit and its organization, it is necessary to get better acquainted with Escrivá. He had a program and an ideal: "For me, it is necessary to *hide myself and disappear,* so that the only thing that appears is·what Jesus Christ wanted to be realized in the world."

In the initial stage we can see the style and the significance of everything that followed. To quote again from Berglar, "After the curious experience of 1928, and again after that of 1930, there was no external change whatsoever. Josémaría Escrivá did not act as would most founders of human projects. Such people usually make declarations and present proposals explaining their motives, means, goals, and immediate plans. Constantly concerned about their public image, they try to stir up interest with press releases. The birth and development of Opus Dei was nothing like this. Its founder did not promulgate any written document in which he expounded, for example, upon the general situation of Spain's Christianity, current problems in the Roman Catholic Church, or the steps that he believed should be taken to promote full Christian dedication among the laity."

> *"For me, it is necessary to hide myself and disappear, so that the only thing that appears is Jesus Christ."—Escrivá*

The German historian continues: "[The young priest] did not found an association to put these principles into practice, nor did he draw up statutes for a proposed organization.... Opus Dei grew as all living things grow, as all things that are not built according to a blueprint are built: it grew silently and slowly, as a plant first breaks through from a seed."

This prevalence of life over theory allowed the seed to grow, day by day, uniting love with experience. And it characterizes Opus Dei to this day. Perhaps it is one of the secrets of its success in the world–and in the Church. This organic growth expands with the slow but relentless rhythm of normal daily life, moving from man to man, from like to like, without debates, manuals, committees, proclamations, ideologies. It moves with what the founder called "the apostolate of friendship and confidence," which is unseen, makes little noise, and never neglects the day to day and the personal. (Some people see this as a sort of secret activity covering up an occult purpose.)

No member of Opus Dei, however infused with apostolic zeal, will ring doorbells and try to distribute propaganda, as do the Jehovah's Witnesses, or seek to entice strangers with standard advertising methods. The doctrinal formation received in the Prelature does not condone this kind of religious promotion. It looks, instead, to the testimony of life as lived, and afterward to the friendship and confidence which are born in the environment of personal relationships. Thus this apostolate is largely invisible, and that is why those who don't understand its meaning confuse it with conspiratorial concealment.

The founder also defined the Work as "a disorganized organization" to explain the character of what organization there is, which I personally experienced. Every place where the men and women of Opus Dei work functions smoothly and soberly; and yet it makes all possible allowance for the unpredictability, complexity, and richness of life, unfettered by intellectual schemes, programs, and ideological cages.

Another biographer of Don Escrivá writes as follows: "Even at the distance of decades, his memory did not fail him and enabled him to recall the *most minute particulars, especially regarding persons, their families, and the events of their households.*" I have emphasized the final words because probably the most disquieting characteristic of the intellectual ideologies which have devastated the last two centuries is the obsession with the universal while neglecting the personal dimension. It gives total attention to ideas and ignores individuals. The founder of Opus Dei, by contrast, was interested in the most minute particulars regarding persons and their families.

CHAPTER SIX

THE STRANGENESS OF NOT BEING STRANGE

IF WE WANT TO understand not only the origin of this Work but also its nature, its present condition, and its possible future, we must search further into the way it was born.

To begin with, reason too is a divine gift and ought not be neglected, leaving to mystery what is proper to it. With this in mind, is it possible to exercise a reasonable faith that the Work is "the result of a divine intervention in history?"

The Church, in fact, has officially declared this to be its origin after the exhaustive documentation required in such cases. This recognition is no marginal fact. If the Church made a mistake—confusing a hallucinator with a true mystic or a conscious deceiver—huge problems would arise. But of course it *cannot* make a mistake because faith speaks of a "special assistance from the Holy Spirit" to avoid this type of disastrous error. Even the opponents of the beatification of Escrivá within the Church have to accept this papal decision if they wish to remain within the Church.

But what about outside the Church? On the level of facts, nothing can be excluded *a priori,* least of all "extraterrestrial interventions" into the affairs of the world. In this respect, the believer is much more open than the nonbeliever, for the latter in principle excludes a whole number of things that do not fit into the theoretical and biased schema which he has accepted as valid for all situations.

On the objective and factual level, then, there is much reason for trust. Above all, there is the solid character of Escrivá. For over a half century, he displayed a concrete realism, enterprising spirit, and iron will, united to a strong religious nature. Like many other saints he was a mystic, but with feet firmly planted on the ground, a contemplative and an organizer, a spiritual man with a degree in canon law.

Is Opus Dei "the result of a divine intervention in history?"

Nothing here, including his family upbringing, would suggest a visionary. His religious style, moreover, had a healthy distrust of the ecstatic devotionalism that chases after visions, supernatural events, prophecies, and ostentatious prodigies.

Don Escrivá's religious beliefs were clear and simple. He used to say that he never doubted for even a moment the truth of the Gospel. His faith, to use his own words, was a gift "so thick you could cut it with a knife."

Perhaps it was owing to this very certainty—he who secretly doubts must seek supporting arguments—that he always preferred and recommended the sort of lay naturalness that led him to cultivate a *piedad sin beatería,* a "piety without bigotry."

This has been well explained by Rafael Gomez Perez, a professor of anthropology at the University of Madrid, a well-known writer in Spanish-speaking countries, and a numerary: "The founder of Opus Dei often used an expression to explain the normal civil life of the members of the Prelature: *lo raro de no ser raros,* 'the strangeness of not being strange.' The normal, usual life of the members of Opus Dei does not express [those] attitudes that can be called 'very religious' according to the contemporary stereotype. The Opus Dei style has nothing to do with anything showy or 'fundamentalist.' Religious images do not cover the walls of the house of a married supernumerary.... Priests do not make frequent visits to their homes, at least not priests of the Prelature; practices of Christian life (such as reciting the Rosary) are not imposed but simply proposed, beginning with the family members. They are never put on display." We should not forget the warning Jesus himself gave: "When you pray, do not be like the hypocrites, who love to stand up in the synagogues and in the plazas, to be visited by people" (Mt. 6, 5).

"Here," Perez continues, "from the very beginning of the Work, the style is that of a family's home. Just as the connection with Opus Dei implies a renewed, voluntary commitment (if you don't want to continue, you simply leave), the atmosphere of a Center is like that of a very harmonious family."

In my own experience, I have never observed in Opus Dei the obsessions with food, with those dietetic taboos that are characteristic of a sectarian or religious fanatic. This ill suits a follower of Jesus, who taught that what contaminates a man does not come from without. (In one rather prestigious church a schism erupted because they could not agree whether tea, coffee, and cocoa should be considered drugs in the biblical sense.)

In Opus Dei, you eat and drink what you please within the limits prescribed by the Church; it is your personal responsibility to pursue the cardinal virtue of temperance. Here, too, is occasion to obey the Gospel precept: "When you fast, do not have a gloomy face like the hypocrites, who disfigure their faces to make people see they are fasting.... When you fast, perfume your head and wash your face, so that people do not see that you are fasting, but only your Father in Heaven" (Mt. 6, 16). And horror of horrors, in Opus Dei, if you really want to smoke, you may.

An episode in the life of Blessed Josémaría, apparently trivial but to me profoundly significant, gives even more scandal to our contemporary intolerant moralists. On June 25, 1944, the archbishop of Madrid ordained the first three priests of Opus Dei. All three were engineers and would henceforth be able to lighten the load of work placed on Monsignor Escrivá's shoulders—the spiritual formation of members. On the afternoon of their ordination, the founder asked if any of the new priests used tobacco, to which they all replied in the negative.

And what did that excellent man do? Remember, Jesus Christ was an enemy of Puritans and Phariseeism; remember too the old saying, "He who hates vices, hates men." What Escrivá said was, if no one smoked, at least one should start doing so. In other words, Escrivá wanted normal people. He wanted people ready to make any sacrifice—one of his teachings was that "mortifications should mortify yourself, and not others"—but he also wanted a common outside appearance. And since normality at the time meant smoking—at least half the adult population smoked—this too should be done by his followers.

This normality, which even the outsider notices in the men and women of the Work, is the direct fruit of the Escrivá tree. He also recommended that his members not long for anything miraculous, since the greatest miracle of all was life itself, and the daily work which the Christian is called to sanctify. As he puts it in *The Forge,* No. 60: "Each day be conscious of your duty to be a saint. A saint! And that doesn't mean doing strange things. It means a daily struggle in the interior life and in heroically fulfilling your duty right through to the end."

It is significant that in the cause of the beatification, Opus Dei did not follow the traditional method which does research into miracles, prodigies, inexplicable facts, and divine gifts.

When I studied the documents, I found that the research had concentrated on the practice of Christian and human virtues more than on its mystery; and these virtues are all the more heroic the more they are ordinary and not ostentatious. It seemed to confirm that the founder too was normal, as he wanted Opus Dei as a whole to be, even with his radical commitment to the Gospel.

When everything has been examined, there would seem to be no reason to suspect that Opus Dei is falsely claiming to have its origin in a mysterious event. And this initial event is isolated; not the first in a series. The Work, moreover, is the sworn enemy of all ostentation, whether collective or individual. As the official statutes say, *Gloria Operis Dei est sine humana gloria vivere* ("The glory of Opus Dei is to live without human glory"); if there is any glory, it should remain hidden, *in interiore hominis,* in the intimacy of a home, of a family, within the four walls of a place of work. The Work's reputation for secrecy is intensified by this avoidance of anything that attracts attention, such as shouting about miracles or prophetic gifts.

Then, too, there is the reserve of Escrivá in speaking about the event. He spoke of it only rarely and when pressed, and he said only that he "saw" something and never gave any details. And he always recalled that the mission as revealed to him appeared to be more a burden to accept with obedience than a much-coveted reward or crown of personal mystical search.

He never supported his authority as founder upon this charismatic event, nor did he ever use it as leverage to increase his prestige, to attract members, or to counter the many obstacles that were put in his way within the Church. On the contrary: if he ever needed to refer to it—always with his own followers, and in response to their precise questions—he encouraged them not to go into too much depth about it. In sum, he presented it as an objective event which surprised him, as a constraint and *not* as a privilege that had been granted him by God. He was thoroughly

convinced that the beginning of the adventure had been something *extraordinary*, but once under way, his duty was to pay
attention to the *ordinary*—to help people discover all the hidden
potentialities of normal life.

Peter Berglar confirms: "He was always extremely sober in
speaking about mystical graces or charisma. This mode of acting
was much more than a natural characteristic: it reveals the authenticity of the gifts he had received. Whoever talks about a mystical
or extraordinary encounter with God encourages doubts about its
authenticity."

The Crusaders' cry, *Deus vult!* ("God wants it"), was probably an
illusion. The tragic story that followed, ending in glory, blood, and
defeat, heroism and failure, sacrifice and
avarice, seems to show that God did not
want it. But in the case of Opus Dei,
much seems to show (at least to human
eyes) that this time God's will was not an
illusion, that the Christian God, toward
the end of the second millennium, really
wanted to have a work that would be his
own, that He truly called sons and
daughters to share in it from every part of the world.

*Escrivá firmly
believed his duty was
to pay attention to
the ordinary—to help
people discover all the
hidden potentialities
of normal life.*

The skepticism, perplexity, irony, doubts, and negations of
those who are outside are not really important. What counts is the
certainty of those who are inside, and this is what gives the Work
its energy and extraordinary power. And I can guarantee, based on
what I have seen and intuited, that the Work is not characterized
by any crusading fanaticism.

But despite its lack of fanaticism—such as refusing to condemn
alcohol, coffee, tobacco, or chocolate—there is an element which
clearly distinguishes the Work from the sectarian mentality that
is driven by an uncritical enthusiasm for the "cause" and for the
group. In this connection, the thought of *Furrow,* No. 870, is

appropriate: "Matters can rarely be resolved by aggressive polemics which humiliate people. And things are certainly never cleared up when there is a fanatic among those arguing the case."

But if I did not find a fanatic in the Work, I did find Christians who, unlike some contemporary clerical intelligentsia, do not consider it an illness to cultivate a reasonable enthusiasm for discovering the horizons of faith. These people have decided to live this very thing—the faith—and to offer to others, beginning with those closest to them, the joy which they have experienced. And they don't intend to compromise on this. Listen to a point presented in *The Forge,* No. 131: "To give way in matters of faith would be a false charity.... This is not fanaticism, but quite simply the practice of our faith. It does not entail disliking anyone. *We can give way in all accidental matters, but in matters of faith we cannot give way.*"

These Christians are convinced that it is a great privilege—to which they correspond with the maximum effort—of having been called by the grace of God to take part in an adventure that arose not from the will of man but from the will of God.

This powerful impulse grew from the certainty that on October 2, 1928, God unexpectedly tolled His bell, and a young priest from a remote and insignificant Spanish town "saw" what He wanted to be realized.

It is this certainty that animates the Work; it is this certainty that cannot be damaged by any human dialectic; it is this certainty that has now been confirmed by Christ Himself through His vicar on earth, the Pope. It is my easy prediction, that Opus Dei will not play a small role in the future of the Church.

Having considered the modes and possibilities of that event in 1928, it is time to learn more of its content.

CHAPTER SEVEN

A RELIGIOUS REALITY

JUST AS WITH THE description of the event, so now with the substance of what this chosen man, Don Escrivá, *saw:* We will go to the official terms employed in the Postulation of the Cause of Beatification:

"God was calling him to dedicate his whole life to the service of the Church through the promotion of this supernatural reality that would later be called Opus Dei. The purpose for which the Lord brought this kind of supernatural reality into existence was for people of all walks of life—beginning with intellectuals in order to reach everyone eventually—with a specific vocation from God, and, conscious of the greatness of the Christian vocation, to pursue sanctity and to exercise an apostolate in the world, among companions and friends, each in one's own milieu, profession and work, without change of state."

We need to pay attention to all the words, especially, *"The purpose for which the Lord brought this kind of supernatural reality into existence...."* For if we do not take this seriously, we cannot pretend to understand Opus Dei or, for that matter, any other expression of Catholicism, of any kind, at any age, beginning with the Church herself. What many "intelligent" people seem to have forgotten for decades is a clear necessity: *religious experience* must be approached with *religious categories.*

In the case of Opus Dei, its social manifestations speak for themselves, but if you want to understand its essence, you must try to imagine what a spiritual experience, an experience of faith, would be like.

But note: I do not intend to defend everything and everybody. Not a little of the distrust and hostility that surround religious organizations are often justified. To be "a man of the Church" does not automatically overcome the huge mass of sin and the limits of every human life. So many distrusts and hostilities, which burden the Work especially, have their origin in inadequate methods of interpretation.

Religious experience must be approached with religious categories.

A religious reality—and something that does not intend to be anything but radically, and essentially, religious, like Opus Dei— almost always winds up being analyzed and then judged according to political, economic, or sociological categories. Important categories, but categories that exhaust the realities of politics, the economy, and society.

A reality like the Work of Don Escrivá certainly has political relevance, at least in the etymological sense of the word, in the sense of having influence on the *polis* (the city). Or, better, it is not so much the Work itself that has this relevance but the persons who have been religiously formed by it. Christianity, after all, is founded on the incarnation of God in human history. Therefore, nothing that is human is foreign to the Gospel.

Yet the most relevant sociopolitical consequences of the actions of a person of faith are nothing but the consequences of the choice for faith. For this, adequate categories need to be observed, or at least taken into account.

Baruch Spinoza (1632–1677) taught that "the actions of men are not to be laughed at or scorned, but understood." What then is the cause of those kinds of behavior that do not seek to explain other kinds of activity?

In a corporation, people unite for economic ends; in a political party, they do so for political ends; in a club, in an association, in a sports club, they join with one another to pursue recreational, cultural, social, or athletic purposes. Their motivations are legitimate and often admirable. But they are human motives. This is not the case for a religious reality—for a Roman Catholic one in particular, like Opus Dei.

Begin with the words at the start: *"The purpose for which the Lord brought this supernatural reality into existence...."* And now consider the words that precede and follow the attempt to describe the reality as "seen" by the young Don Josémaría. Opus Dei is defined as *"a specific calling by God"* and *"the search for sanctity."*

Could anyone suspect the leadership of the Work, of its establishment, or the founder himself of a cynical hypocrisy, of being whitened sepulchers who have built a religious facade over human interests, who have thrown a devout cloak over worldly goals such as power or wealth?

I really cannot see what allurements of money and social prestige could have induced me to lead a life like that of Don Josémaría Escrivá for half a century, whether priest or lay. I would not be able to follow that path for earthly motives alone.

Yet the life can be among the most joyous there is. In *The Forge,* 1006, the founder wrote: "I see the formula with crystal clarity, the secret of happiness, both earthly and eternal. It is not just a matter of accepting the Will of God but of embracing it, of identifying oneself with it—in a word, of loving the Divine Will with a positive act of our own will. I repeat, this is the infallible secret of joy and peace."

Based on the testimonies I have collected, this "secret of happiness" appears to be functioning well. But *only* under the conditions Escrivá indicates here. And these are not human conditions.

The *conditio sine qua non* is to believe in the Will of God, and not in our will which seeks joy, happiness, and peace without a transcendent perspective, and which plans, actually, to bring us not paradise on earth so much as an everyday purgatory or hell.

But then what about those at the headquarters at Viale Bruno Buozzi who work alongside the prelate and who preside over the General Counsel (for the men) and the Central Advisory (for the women)? They are always changing positions, since apart from the prelate, nobody has a lifetime post in the Work, and there are no internal careers. After holding any administrative post, each one returns to the professional work or trade he had before, without having acquired anything but spiritual benefit.

Opus Dei is predominantly popular among laborers and campesinos in Spain and Latin America.

We could also speculate about those others who govern the "regions" that dot the world—the name of the parts into which the Work is divided. These people could be unscrupulous puppeteers with a devout appearance and in reality dedicated to goals that are far from religious.

And how about the others, the eighty thousand? The majority do not seem to conform to this stereotype. Among the documents furnished by the Prelature to anyone who wants verification are statistics about the educational level, income, and social status of the members. These documents show a predominance of middle-to-low levels in all categories. In Spain and Latin America, for example, Opus Dei is predominantly popular among laborers and *campesinos*.

The story of the South American taxi driver is one example. He was amazed when, after asking for admission to the Work, he discovered that the organization included professionals, executives, and intellectuals. On the basis of his experience, he thought that the Work was reserved for modest laborers like himself.

But whatever the socio-economic level of the members, the fact remains that their choice and their life are incomprehensible to someone who does not realize that religious experience—*authentic* religious experience—not only exists but is one of the most powerful forces there is, able to move mountains. It is a gratuitous and renewable energy that has changed history and will continue to change history. This is probably history's secret motor, even if it has not been discerned by those who believe religion is for the gullible.

The average Marxist deceives himself into thinking he understands everything by attributing all human action to an economic force. Many disciples of psychoanalysis believe they hold the key to the human enigma by attributing everything to sexual impulses. And every modern ideology sees everything in political terms of "right" and "left," of "conservative" and "progressive," with their clashing interests. This distortion has also infected wide strata of the Catholic world. This accounts in large part for the hostility, lay as well as clerical, toward a reality as religious as Opus Dei.

Augusto Del Noce, the perceptive philosopher/believer, told me in an interview a few years before his death: "For centuries of Catholic thought, the interpretative scheme for both past and present was that of *faith/heresy, religion/secular, devotion/godlessness, sacred/profane,* and *high/low.* Now, with the adoption of a certain modernity, the outlook for many people of the Church has become *progressivist/conservative, left/right, revolution/reaction.* Thus a religious interpretation of history has been replaced by a political one. In place of the traditional categories of *true/false, or of good/bad,* we have *progressivist liberal left* (the new saint) and *reactionary right-wing traditionalist* (the sinner).

He continued: "In the new scale of values of certain clerics, the true enemy is not the irreligious one, the blasphemer, or the godless.... The real enemy has become the integrist, that is, the Catholic who wants to take his faith seriously, transforming it from a mere humanitarian sentiment, or 'shared value,' into a guiding vision for all his activity."

The philosopher concluded: "Because of this, even in the Church there is an aversion for the new movements which are seen as 'integrist' and thus destructive; they are the enemy par excellence of this Neochristianity which has shifted from religious to political perspectives, from categories of faith to categories of sociology and economics."

Augusto Del Noce places Opus Dei among the most significant of these movements, even if it is not technically a movement.

This analysis helps to explain the origin of so much hostility. It most likely arises from the application of political categories to a religious reality. This erroneous perspective, which began outside the Church and has fully penetrated it, impedes not so much the acceptance of Opus Dei as the effort to understand what constitutes the *true reality* of Opus Dei. Only then can one consider the consequences for society, politics, and the economy.

This true reality, since it is religious reality, is far from those labels of right or left, of progressive or conservative. These labels are totally inappropriate when we speak about faith, when we are concerned with someone who, "by a special vocation from God" became "conscious of the grandeur of the Christian vocation"— the words the Prelature used in requesting the beatification of its founder.

CHAPTER EIGHT

"STAY WHERE YOU ARE":
ORA ET LABORA

WHAT DO THEY DO, these men and women—of every age, nationality, and social condition—if their special calling to live the Christian vocation in all its grandeur is to adopt the Opus Dei method?

The women and men do not have to do anything other than believe in the truth of the vision granted to that young Spanish priest, Don Escrivá. To take this first step is to join in a project willed by God Himself; to go further, of course, one must accept the "spiritual service agency" that the Prelature is, and its efficacy.

Someone once noted that "the man of today appears ready to understand everything—everything except what is too simple." As a man of today, I did not understand Opus Dei at the beginning of my investigation—not until I realized that the reason for my difficulty was probably that it was too simple.

Perhaps I can help you to understand by going step by step and explaining in elementary terms the life of Opus Dei.

There are hundreds of millions of persons (about nine hundred million) who, having received Baptism in the Catholic Church, are considered Catholic. It is the most numerous religious community on earth, and at present the only religious community with members in practically all the regions of the earth.

In this enormous entity, not everyone takes advantage of this sacramental sign, this indelible mark known as baptism: many, in fact, have no appreciation of it and, in some instances, are even in revolt against it. Others—perhaps a large quantity—are neither enthusiastic nor opposed, taking neither the time nor the opportunity to stand firmly one way or the other. Apparently indifferent, they ask the Church only for certain "services"—whether because of conviction, tradition, or superstition—at certain fundamental stages of life, such as baptisms, weddings, funerals, or a Midnight Mass to get that "Christmas feeling" or because it brings back memories of childhood.

But there is another third group for whom baptism is all-important and truly what the Catechism says it is: an insertion into that Mystical Body of Christ which, according to the words of St. Paul as developed by theological reflection, is the Church; an entrance, that is to say, into the People of God, who believe that they have been redeemed by the Cross on Golgotha and have been called to resurrection to eternal life; a reception of the rights and a shouldering of the responsibilities of being a Christian. These persons, in other words, have been moved by the desire to draw good from their faith, as they have in past centuries and will continue to do in the future.

Beginning in the late twenties, Don Escrivá constantly sent a message to people like this, and through them, to the indifferent or hostile, which I will state in my own words, but which is based on his concepts as I have understood them: "God Himself has decided to make me understand something, and if I can't explain why He chose me, I assure you that I really 'saw' it and am constrained to tell you about it; that is, the time has come to make an end to a Christianity of first and second levels. The Church is not split into professionals of the Gospel on the one side (priests, brothers, sisters, monks, nuns, some lay people) and on the other a huge majority of dilettante Christians, the simple laity, the common faithful—in a word, all of you. The Gospel, *all* the Gospel, is for *all*. God is asking everyone to become a saint, that is, to live the Gospel in its entirety. I know the word saint scares you, because it has become too closely linked to extraordinary people and extraordinary enterprises which seem always to be beyond our reach. But it is not so; it cannot be. I assure you that the God of Jesus Christ is asking each Christian to become perfect, and this perfection, with his grace, ought to be possible for all. If that were not so, why would He have asked it of us? Why would the Gospels quote Jesus as saying to all: 'Be ye perfect, even as your Father in heaven is perfect' "?

"In addition to being a saint, everyone is called to become an apostle."—Escrivá

Continue with the words of Escrivá: "In addition to being a saint, everyone is called to become an *apostle.* That is, to have Christian hope and hand on the message of that Gospel to brothers and sisters. We must try to live it in its fullness; this pertains not only to missionaries or preachers, those professionals of the faith I spoke to you about. For the struggle for sanctity—which is indispensable, since one cannot give what one does not have—is necessarily accompanied by the urge to communicate the secret of your joy to others, if you are truly convinced that God is the Father of all, and that each one of us has been loved and ought to respond to that love with love."

"Very edifying," was the customary reply, even within the Church. "Very fine, but how can it be done? Sanctity and apostolate, at least in the full senses of these words, cannot be achieved or done by everyone, for since the overwhelming majority of Christians have a job, a family, and a great number of obligations, an excessive spiritual effort simply cannot be demanded of them. What can and should be asked of them is to do the best they can in their own situation, perhaps easing the pressure of daily preoccupations so as to dedicate more time to the practices of piety."

But for a fully Christian life, for a true struggle for sanctity, something is needed that they cannot do—leave their way of life and follow not only the precepts of the Church that are expected of all the faithful, but also the evangelical counsels: chastity, poverty, and obedience. They would need, in other words, to enter into one of those institutions which we call Institutes of Perfection and to become religious. This, of course, is impossible for an everyday Christian. Baptism is not enough for such choices, a special vocation is required, which by definition is not, and cannot be, for all.

As for an apostolate, here, too, we are realists. The proclamation of the Gospel requires study, preparation, charisma, and an official position. It is not just inconvenient, it is downright dangerous to ask every Christian to become a missionary. *Unicuique suum* ("to each his own"); and the special task of the laity is to help the missionaries, parish priests, and preachers with their prayers and offerings; helping those, in sum, who are delegated within the Church to this essential and delicate service, which cannot be done by everybody.

This was Don Escrivá's reply: "I think that the path of the 'special' rigorous vocation—the one that leads to the convent, the monastery, the priesthood, or the desert—is a blessed one and necessary for the Church. The brothers and sisters, members of the clergy, consecrated lay people, and such have been a constant and indispensable presence, and they will continue to be. The vows of poverty, chastity, and obedience of the traditional religious state are an unambiguous eschatological sign for the Church and for all humanity, by making present what the Last Things will bring.

"But this minority of baptized men and women, although neces-sary and beneficial, does not have a monopoly on perfection in the design of God, nor on the sanctity and apostolate which sponta-neously follow upon such perfection. I have the duty to proclaim that all Christians can, and should, sanctify themselves in ordinary life, through ordinary things, without having to change one's job, or leave one's family, or renounce the common occupations and pre-occupations of an everyday person. This is to act as did the first Christian generations, who, on the outside, in no way differed from their pagan contemporaries. They took seriously the exhortation of Paul, who anxiously repeated three times in First Corinthians: 'Let everyone continue to live in the condition assigned to him by the Lord, and just as God has called him.' This is the message of Opus Dei—to become holy and be an apostle right where he or she is."

To help understand this still better, listen to a homily of Don Escrivá: "Our lay, secular spirituality is directed to Christians of every condition who, existing in the world, or, better, belonging to the world, are common lay people who aspire to Christian perfec-tion by a divine vocation. Our vocation makes it possible for our secular condition, our ordinary work, our situation in the world, to become the unique means for our sanctification and apostolate."

He qualified this as follows: "We have not assumed our lay, or 'civil,' profession as a masquerade for our apostolic work: it is the same occupation we would have had if we had not joined Opus Dei, it is the same work we will have if we ever incur the misfor-tune of abandoning our vocation." And in conclusion: "We, my sons and daughters, are *people of the street.* And when we work in temporal affairs, we do so not because we are unable to leave them and devote ourselves to religious practices, but because this is our post, this is the place where we encounter Jesus Christ, the place where our vocation has found us and where it will leave us."

In the vision of October 2, 1928, Don Escrivá understood a truth he defined "as *old* as the Gospel and as *new* as the Gospel":

the relevance to eternity of daily activity, seemingly so ephemeral and often considered so irrelevant from a human perspective; the sanctification of the world "from the inside," carried out without leaving the world, and through work itself.

Any work, from the most humble to the most exalted, is good, as long as it is honest work. The atmosphere of freedom that the Gospel brings not only relieves man from the hundreds of precepts (the do's and don'ts) of the Hebraic Law, but also cancels and makes void the list of "shameful" or "religiously dangerous" occupations. As Joachim Jeremias, the great German biblical scholar, observed in his *Jerusalem in the Time of Jesus,* "The first impression one gets in studying the Rabbinic lists is that there is very little room left for honest occupations, since so many were considered dishonorable in ancient Israel." These include: donkey driver, camel driver, sailor, shepherd, shopkeeper, butcher, herald, diver, goldsmith, mason, traveling salesman, tailor, collector of duties, and, according to some, even physician and barber. But the New Testament declaration that "it is not for you to call anything profane, which God has made clean" (Acts 10, 15) recovers the dignity, and the *sanctity,* of all labor.

In the words of Rafael Gomez Perez: "In the spirit of Opus Dei, there are no prohibited professions, except for those that are outside the bounds of Christian morality, and thus of human morality. Neither commercial nor financial nor even political occupations are disallowed, despite the commonplaces about how difficult it is to exercise these professions and still be moral. According to the spirit of Opus Dei, it is not merely a question of being honest in these or other professions, but of living them *in a supernatural sense.* And that means being sanctified in them."

And therefore it is precisely work—the vital center, the very heart not only of the legitimate interests of men, but of their personal and social passions—that makes the whole proposition so efficacious, and provides almost limitless perspectives for the future. This is the reality that Don Escrivá found "new" in appearance but "old" in reality—as old, that is to say, as the book of Genesis: "The Lord God took man and placed him in the Garden of Eden, in order that he cultivate it and tend it [*ut operaretur*]" (2, 15).

Here, in this one small verse of the Bible, lies something of decisive importance that has been little noted by Christian theology—perhaps it has been ignored through forces both internal and external to the Church. These words of the second chapter of the first book of the Judeo-Christian Scriptures occur *before* the Fall; they are *antecedent* to the original sin of Adam and Eve. Thus in the words of Dominique Le Tourneau, priest of the Prelature and a long-time collaborator of the founder: "Labor is an essential part of God's plan for man, it is a *natural* function which the Creator willed for His creature, even before any estrangement arose between them. *It is only the fatiguing aspect of human activity that results from the punishment for Original Sin. Work, in itself, is a good and noble thing.*"

"**Work, in itself, is a good and noble thing.**"

And didn't Jesus of Nazareth Himself make this clear (as Escrivá elaborates) by spending long periods of his life preaching not with his words but with his daily life—his obscure, patient profession of carpentry in a village of Galilee?

Escrivá said that "work is the means by which man participates in the divine work of the Creation. God willed that His own work be brought to completion every day by the hands of man. Thus man is called to be a co-creator in his work." Hence, among other things, the meaning of the name Opus Dei, which is not that the Work is of God in the sense of some copyright but rather in the sense of an *operatio Dei,* "of doing the work of God," the work that every man and woman is called to do.

The history of spirituality, like any other history, *non facit saltus* ("does not make leaps"). And Escrivá himself in his holy honesty recognized that he had been given to understand clearly the salvific value of daily life, of which work is such a large part, because he had come along at the right moment and had found the right conditions for understanding and applying the idea. It was the result of experience and reflection on what the Gospel itself proposed.

Understand that the *fatigue* of work has been confused by many theologians and spiritual writers with *work itself*. They consider work as a sentence, or expiation of sin, and not as an essential component of God's plan in creating the world and the world's inhabitants. Alternatively, work is not considered as a good in itself, but rather as a good for the spiritual life, as an ascetic means of combatting idleness, the father of all vices—work can overcome sloth and acedia, and all the temptations that accompany them.

A similar conception of the use of work came to a high point in the famous and perhaps legendary anecdote about Paul the Hermit. Paul the Hermit, who lived in Egypt in the second to third centuries A.D., did not need to work to support himself—he lived on the produce of a tiny garden—but he made himself weave baskets of reeds in order not to be idle. At the end of every month, he piled up all the baskets and burned them.

Yet other spiritual thinkers have criticized secular preoccupations—above all, labor—as an obstacle to contemplation, to reflection upon the mysteries of God and ascetical practices.

This gave birth during the Middle Ages to the religious orders that were significantly called "mendicant," or "begging" orders. As one historian put it, "[The theologians of the mendicant orders] affirmed the nonobligatory character of manual activity; not to be sure, out of sloth, but to give witness to their poverty and faith in God's providence."

Now history, according to the profoundly Christian outlook of Benedetto Croce, "is not essentially *just* but only *justifying*." We should not forget that "the social structures of the early medieval period and for much of the following periods (feudal at first, and later marked by division into distinct social classes) made it very difficult to recognize any salvific value in the personal labor of each person, since individuals were not of interest as such, but only as members of the various categories that made up civil society. It was a hierarchical society, with a continuity of honor, prestige, and possessions based above all on hereditary transmission. Hence a mentality was formed that considered labor a kind of *dishonor,* or at least deprived of any profound value. On the other hand, the message about the sanctification of work is easily intelligible in an epoch like our own, which considers the professional competence of individual persons as the foundation of social organization."

In any case, the Protestant Reformation did not improve the situation—it aggravated it. According to Dominique Le Tourneau, "In the sixteenth century, the Lutheran schism from Rome which led to Protestantism delayed the discovery of the sanctifying value of work. Opposed to work was the Protestant conception of Original Sin as the radical corruption of human nature, and the refusal on the part of the reformers to attribute any salvific value to the works of man, even if completed in a state of grace."

The pious Protestant may have devoted himself, over the ages, to work of one sort or the other, but he was not convinced that this work had any value in the eyes of God. There was much work in the Protestant world, but not the joy of knowing that one was doing the will of God, or collaborating with Him in creation. Nor do many lay people in the Catholic Church have the right view of work. For the religious, ideas about work are necessarily different.

Saint Thomas à Kempis, for example, in his *Imitation of Christ,* writes: "To eat, drink, be awake, sleep, rest or labor and to be subject to all the other necessities of nature: all this cannot but be called *misery* for the devout soul who would like to be completely detached and free from all sin." But recall that he is writing a book about monastic formation, about a cloistered spirituality.

Escrivá clearly and constantly asserts in his writing that the Church would always need these special vocations.

"We do not exist in *opposition* to the spirituality of the religious," Escrivá would say. "Our flower is a *different* one, growing out of the same perennial richness of the Gospel."

Among other things, this clears Escrivá of harboring an obsession that excludes any idea or system other than his own, from the elitist belief that one is God's elect, Heaven's sole authority on earth. He understands all too well that the dynamism of the Catholic Church includes various vocations and charisms. According to the teaching of Christ Himself, "There are many rooms in the House of God," and each person is called in one of many ways, all of which are legitimate.

A mistake of much Catholic spirituality was the attempt to have all the baptized live a spirituality that God envisioned for only a few, the few called to the cloisters. Many present-day Christians have seen the problem and have searched for an answer. But the observation of Cardinal Albino Luciani, the future John Paul I, says it best: "Some well-intentioned authors have tried to propose a *spirituality for lay people,* as if it were a 'pocket edition,' adapted and corrected, and less demanding, than the spirituality for the 'perfect', for the religious and members of the clergy. But Opus Dei has proposed, for the first time, a *lay spirituality.* And this is truly autonomous, *different* from the clerical spirituality which is right and advisable for those who are called to it, but not for everyday Christians."

These latter, according to Escrivá, should not be forced to be "perfect" (as the Gospel asks) *in spite of* their profession or their trade, but rather *by means of it* and *thanks to it,* however mundane it may appear. Because there is no work, or practically no work, which cannot be sanctified, and in which one cannot be sanctified.

One must remain where one is, and in that place "search out sanctity and exercise an apostolate among friends and companions, in one's own profession and in one's own work, *without changing one's state of life.*" Or, as Escrivá also put it, "I do not tell you that you can be sanctified *despite* the fact that you are a lay person, a simple baptized Christian who lives and labors in the world. I tell you that you can—and ought—to be sanctified *precisely because* you are that."

Hence the motto which synthesizes the content of Escrivá's vision: "Sanctify work; sanctify yourself in the perfect carrying out of your work; and sanctify others through your work"; that is, through missionary activity and apostolate.

This is something far beyond the traditional spirituality for the lay person. It lifts work out of the rut of being only part of the person, viewed principally as a series of duties to be carried out without any real spirituality or theology of labor. This view considers work nothing but a harsh necessity of life, an exercise of Christian virtue necessary to get through this vale of tears.

> *"Sanctify work; sanctify yourself in the perfect carrying out of your work; and sanctify others through your work."—Escrivá*

Escrivá, on the other hand, speaks of the "unity of life," the need not only to overcome but also to eliminate the double life, the traditional schizophrenia of Catholic lay people torn between the desire for perfection, which implies estrangement from the world, and the need to remain in the world to fulfill family and professional obligations.

Opus Dei proclaims that there is no reason why the Christian should leave the world, that the lay person himself *is* "the world," and that the world is saved from within, not from without. It is like saying that the leaven which is in the dough, by being a part of the dough itself, makes the dough rise from the inside.

In the last few decades, well-intentioned members of the more open religious organizations have been theorizing about the necessity of going out to the world, of getting closer to those who work. This is excellent, says Don Escrivá, but it still presupposes a movement from *outside* toward the *inside.* It is not this way with Opus Dei. There, you remain where you are, you do not leave, even in a psychological sense, the place where you are sanctified and where you sanctify others.

"Opus Dei is not the ultimate stage of desacralizing or of making religious sisters or brothers, and priests, *more worldly:* we do not have to become *more like the others,* because the others are lay people like ourselves, only in need of help in discovering that their ordinary life can be the place where eternal beatitude can be prepared for each person"—words spoken by the Blessed Josémaría.

For a still better understanding here is another statement of his from 1968: "I am really hoping for the day when the phrase *Catholics are penetrating into diverse social environments* will no longer be in circulation, and everybody will recognize that it is a clerical expression. This has nothing to do with the apostolate of Opus Dei. Its members have no need of 'penetrating' into temporal structures because of the simple fact that they are common citizens, equal to the rest, and because they were already in those structures and will remain in them."

For instance, a lawyer or a laborer are not "members of Opus Dei who have become a lawyer or a laborer," but rather they are "a lawyer and a laborer and in what refers to their spiritual formation, are members of Opus Dei."

And here, in a mix of his quotation, is the decisive point: "Whoever thinks that supernatural life is built up by turning one's back on work, will not understand our vocation: for us, in fact, work is the specific means of sanctification. Our *interior* life [of contemplation in the very heart of the world] flows from— takes its impetus from—each person's *exterior* life of work."

In my view, the celebrated precept of Saint Benedict for his monks could be turned on its head: rather than *ora et labora* ("pray and work," whereby work is juxtaposed to prayer) one should *labora et ora* ("work and pray") so that the office, the factory, the street, the home become themselves a church, a place of prayer. Exterior work ought not to interrupt prayer, just as the beating of the heart does not distract us from our activities.

But does this lead to an activism sought for its own sake? Escrivá insisted that "the specific vocation to Opus Dei leads one to transform the ordinary and the normal—which for the great majority of persons is their professional work—into a path where God is encountered: the God of Jesus Christ, from Whom, in this perspective, everything comes and toward which everything ought to tend, and to which the world as a whole ought to be led back, from the inside, by people who are of and 'in' the world, but at the same time are not 'worldly.'"

The Way tells us how to ward off possible danger. For example, No. 81: "Action is worthless without prayer; prayer is worth more with sacrifice"; or No. 82: "First: *prayer.* Then, *atonement.* In the third place—and very much 'in the third place'—action."

And so we are dealing with people who are "of the world" and who remain in that world. But they remain there with a particular spiritual attitude, as an historical document cited earlier makes plain: "To refer to Opus Dei without making explicit mention of dedication to prayer in the midst of daily work and the normality of everyday living, is to deny its essence. Everything—truly *everything*—in the Work is designed to facilitate the encounter of each member with God, through a life of continual prayer."

CHAPTER NINE

A SPIRITUAL AGENCY

✝

TO BE ORIGINAL IN the etymological sense of the word is to go back to the origins. This is what Don Escrivá wanted to do, and in this consists his originality. He said that "the safest way to understand Opus Dei is to think about the life of the first Christians." Everything, finally, can be reduced to a thought of this type: "Have you received baptism? Now, take seriously what that means and be consistent, living according to what the Church proposes, which, by administering the sacrament, has taken you within itself, that is, into that Body of which Christ is the Head. Becoming holy (and you can: everyone can, if they trust in the help of God Who cannot fail, since the perfection of every man, of every woman, is what He explicitly wills) but continuing your customary life; remain where you are, at least in external appearances, with your work and with your personal and professional tasks. Remember that, in faith, all occupations have a great value, no matter how insignificant they might be in the eyes of men; all are of great importance, even if, objectively speaking, they are humble, because this importance depends on the love for God and the love for man that the person doing that task puts into it. Unless it is a special vocation, God does not require strangeness, unusual things, or acts of noisy heroism; you can be called to heroism, yes, but within yourself, in an intimate context, private, and in a 'normal' way. Pray a lot—even always—but without compulsion or exhibitionism, transforming your work, whatever it might be, into prayer, and giving it a supernatural dimension, fulfilling it as well as possible for the love of God and neighbor."

"Pray a lot—even always—but without compulsion or exhibitionism, transforming your work, whatever it might be, into prayer."
—Escrivá

From the search for sanctity arises the need—more than the duty—of apostolate. But this too must be normal, discrete, spontaneous, and quiet, according to the pure style of Christian life from which it ought to flow.

The first ecclesiastical decree approving Opus Dei in 1950 said in part: "The members of Opus Dei exercise the annunciation of the Gospel to their fellows above all *through means of example* which they give to their neighbors, their colleagues and companions at work, in their family, social, and professional lives, *striving always and everywhere to be better*" (italics mine).

A few remarks of the authoritative synthesis given by Dominique Le Tourneau explain the last words of this decree: "Work well done has the force of an example. Christians ought to transform all the perfection of which they are capable, whether on the human plane (professional competence) or on the divine plane (the love of God and the serving of souls), in order that such work become, objectively, a complete job. It will be difficult for us to sanctify a work that is not fully complete, or not perfect. If this fullness is lacking, it will be difficult to attain that necessary professional prestige which Monsignor Escrivá considers 'the cathedra from which others are taught to sanctify their labor and to conform their lives to the demands of the Christian life.' From this follows the need for a continual professional formation, the acquisition, within one's proper field, of all the human knowledge one is capable of acquiring. To be of help to others, each one ought to strive to carry out his own job as well as the best of his colleagues, or, if possible, better than the best."

Among other things, we can begin to see here (and we will return to this point) the origin of the talk about the "power" of the members of Opus Dei. Putting everything into their work, some become outstanding. But *this* professional excellence is the *means of helping others.*

In regard to the members of Opus Dei, the question sooner or later arises: "What is the engine that drives them to be so up-to-date, so competent, so professional?" What is the strategy or style of this mission that is at once so domestic, even hidden, and at the same time so extraordinarily effective? We turn again to Don Escrivá: "Work where you are, carrying out completely the duties of your profession or trade and improving every day. Be loyal, generous, and understanding with others, and demanding of yourself. Be mortified and cheerful. This will be your apostolate. And without your knowing why, considering how little you are, the people in your surroundings will seek you out and they will speak to you in a natural, simple way; at the end of the day, in a get-together of family members, neighbors, or what have you, in the bus, or walking...."

The apostolate, as we already know, is one of friendship, of confidence, without pulpits, preaching, rhetoric, abstruse theology—but with the most diligently orthodox Catholicism which is constantly being formed. It consists rather in tête-à-tête chats between two persons, and especially between colleagues, given the centrality of work.

Again, in the words of Escrivá, "Let those words glide, at just the right moment, into the ear of a friend who is wavering; or that conversation that sheds light and provides orientation, which you know how to provoke on purpose; that professional counsel that improves his work; the discrete indiscretion which brings you to suggest unsuspected horizons...."

This then, is the aim, this is the strategy that Opus Dei proposes to Catholics, with all the necessary authorization of the Church, at universal and local levels.

It is a good program for a believer. Yet it appears to hold a fascination even for those outside the Catholic fold, a fact witnessed to by the high percentage of converts.

This can also be seen in the "cooperators" of the Work, defined by an authoritative source as follows: "The cooperators, even though not members of Opus Dei, help the Prelature with their prayers, if they are believers, and with their work or with some form of economic assistance. They form part of their own association, which is inseparable from the Work." And: "Cooperators can be men and women who are non-Catholics, non-Christians, and even nonbelievers, without any religious affiliation. Opus Dei is the first institution in the Church that calls for the organized collaboration of non-Catholics, non-Christians, agnostics, and atheists."

This is another case where the reality does not in the least correspond to the established popular image which sees the Work as an impenetrable sect of fanatic *Katholiks* who have built a fortress around dogmatic decrees, intolerant and closed to all ecumenical efforts. The truth is quite otherwise: it is "the first institution of the Church" which has made a place for all.

The program of the Work, then, is a good one—good from the religious and human perspectives. To have a colleague who tries earnestly to live an ideal like this means, for instance, that if you had a bad car accident and found a mechanic who was a member of Opus Dei, you could be sure of a meticulous repair job at a just price. Not free, of course, not even with a discount. *The Way,* No. 979, is pragmatic: "It is human nature to have little appreciation for what costs but little. That is why I recommended to you *the apostolate of not giving.* Never fail to claim what is fairly and justly due to you from the practice of your profession, even if your profession is the instrument of your apostolate."

A good program, indeed. But if you are convinced, if you think it could work for you, how do you do it? They answer, "Very simply." Go with confidence to the Prestigious Agency of Spiritual Service founded in Madrid in 1928 and based in Rome since 1947, with affiliates all over the world. Contact the agency and put into action (apart from your mysterious and gratuitous vocation) your good will, your willingness to be formed. The agency will take care of the rest.

Thus there seem to have been two things that the young priest discovered in his famous vision: (1) the possibility—even the necessity—of all the baptized to sanctify themselves in their work, whatever it might be, and in their ordinary lives, and the possibility—or the necessity—of being missionaries of their faith, or apostles; and (2) the need to found an institution, an ecclesiastical structure that would enable this program for persons to be realized. The founder labored all his life to create this structure, to make it carry out its purpose as efficiently as possible.

Pippo Corigliano, an engineer from Naples and director of the Information Office of the Prelature in Rome, uses an analogy: "Opus Dei is like a spiritual filling station: whoever wants to can come and get a full tank, and can come back whenever necessary to get the carburetors tuned or have some maintenance work done on his interior life."

The image of the Spiritual Service Agency does not seem different, in substance, from the image of a filling station for souls.

But perhaps the image of an agency is a little closer to the reality than a service station. That image implies that anyone can come along casually, get a fill-up, and never be seen again, without having thanked the service-station attendant nor had any real choice since gasoline is gasoline.

But Opus Dei is not like that. Its doors are open for those who want to leave (the founder said, "If somebody is with us it's because they want to be, which is the purest of spiritual motives") but you have to knock at the door to get in. This shows that it is really the "services" of this agency that people want to profit from, that they are motivated by that enigmatic force in Christian theology called "a vocation."

That this really happens seems to have been demonstrated, among other things, by Corigliano, who said, "A proof that it requires a specific vocation from God consists in the fact that there are thousands of cooperators who have known the Work for ten, twenty, or more years and who contribute generously to the apostolate, and yet do not ask to become members. And this is not because they are not worthy or capable of sanctity, but simply because they follow a different path."

To enter Opus Dei, you must have a proper awareness that spiritual pluralism is a treasure of the Church.

Thus Opus Dei is not a political party, not a club to which you sign up. You can make a request to join only if you have been inspired by a vocation. This vocation is proved not only by cautious initial verifications, but also by the temporary nature of the commitment, which must be renewed every year until the time of a permanent commitment. This mysterious barrier, this vocation, has among other things kept the Work from falling prey to the temptation of exclusivity, as if to be a "real Catholic" you would have to be a disciple of Blessed Josémaría Escrivá.

To enter Opus Dei and stay through a choice that is subjectively free but objectively willed and guided by God, you must have a proper awareness that spiritual pluralism is a treasure of the Church.

Catholicism is unlike Protestantism, which has split into a thousand different groups of Christians. In Catholicism, the hundreds of diverse sensibilities or spiritualities did not become little, disputing churches, but rather fit together like tiles in the multi-colored mosaic that is the Church in the form of orders, congregations, institutes, movements, families, and so on—all recognized, after adequate testing, by the hierarchy. One vocation, but lived in a countless diversity of modes.

CHAPTER TEN
WHO COMES, WHO GOES

✝

BUT HOW CAN YOU "prove" you have a vocation to Opus Dei, the special calling for this way of life?

To paraphrase an official text: "How does someone know if he has received this vocation? The simplest and most common way is when a person, having come in contact through friendship with those who belong to the Prelature, recognizes its spirit and begins to ask himself whether this might be his way, too. The local directors of Opus Dei are the ones who judge if there really are indications of a vocation. It is the Prelature that grants a definitive admission. As in any voluntary organization, Opus Dei reserves the right of admission. There is freedom on both sides, on the part of the one who requests admission, as well as on the part of the Prelature to accept him or not."

But if there is a vocation—or at least indications of one—who can knock on the door? Everyone over eighteen can: men and women—

celibate, betrothed, married, bereaved—of any social condition, nationality, and race. There are not a few aspiring members over eighty years old, "laborers of the last hour," as in the Gospel.

Statistics show that Opus Dei is not an exclusive or elitist group, which only the rich and powerful are asked to join. Cardinal Jaime L. Sin, the archbishop of Manila, has told how in the zones of poverty in the Philippines, Opus Dei not only helps the poor, but accepts many as members. The Work is also popular in the *favelas* and in the *villas miseria* of Latin America. Over half a million pilgrims, poor or of modest means, travel to Torreciudad, shrine built by Opus Dei. Not a few of these humble pilgrims are members of the Work.

Let us hear from the well-informed Gomez Perez, who writes quite objectively, although he is "existentially compromised," as he would put it. "The professional profile of the members responds to the *normality* that is one of the constant features of Opus Dei: a majority of persons with occupations or professions with a middle level income,

Who can knock on the door? Everyone over eighteen can: men and women—celibate, betrothed, married, bereaved.

some with a high income, and a few with a low income. Nevertheless this generalization would not hold true, for example, for some South American, African, or Asian countries, where the economic conditions of life are much poorer. The Work may have a percentage of professional intellectuals that is somewhat higher than usual, especially professors. Therefore, the principal idea that suffices for understanding the rest is this: no profession, no honest trade, no matter how modest, is an obstacle to belonging to Opus Dei. Its social composition, once it has been established in a country, always shows a perfect correspondence with the local situation—so, from brick masons to industrial executives, from farmers to writers. The mere fact of being situated higher than others, according to human categories, does not confer any type of

Blessed Josémaría Escrivá (left) and Fr. Alvaro del Portillo (right) with Pope John XXIII, 1960. At the end of this audience, John XXIII said the spirit of Opus Dei had opened up for him "unexpected horizons of apostolate."

Pope Paul VI greeting Blessed Josémaría Escrivá in 1965 at the ELIS Center, a technical training center located in a working-class section of Rome. The project was begun on the initiative of Pope John XXIII, who decided to devote a sum of money to the creation of a social-work project in Rome and entrusted the entire project to Opus Dei.

From left: Blessed Josémaría, Fr. Alvaro del Portillo, the first successor to the founder as head of Opus Dei, and Fr. Javier Echevarría, who is the current bishop prelate of Opus Dei, in Rome, 1968.

Blessed Josémaría Escrivá with women from different continents, in Rome, 1971.

The founder of Opus Dei undertook many apostolic journeys in which he taught about the Catholic faith. He is seen here before a packed audience in Buenos Aires in 1974.

Pope John Paul II incensing relic of Blessed Josémaría Escrivá during beatification ceremony in St. Peter's Square, May 17, 1992.

St. Peter's Square on May 17, 1992, during the beatification Mass of Msgr. Josémaría Escrivá.

Pope John Paul II greets Bishop Alvaro del Portillo (1914-1994) in St. Peter's Square following a Mass in honor of Blessed Josémaría Escrivá, May 18, 1992.

Facade of St. Peter's Basilica on May 17, 1992, when Pope John Paul II beatified Msgr. Escrivá. Some 300,000 people jammed the square that day for the ceremony. A portrait of Msgr. Escrivá hangs at left.

Bishop Javier Echevarría, Prelate of Opus Dei, Boston, Massachusetts, 1995.

Valle Grande Rural Institute, Canete, Peru. Begun in 1965, this training institute offers courses and seminars in agricultural sciences.

Arnold Hall Conference Center, a center of Opus Dei in Pembroke, Massachusetts.

Pontifical Atheneum of the Holy Cross, Rome, offers degrees in philosophy, theology, canon law and institutional Church communications.

An instructor at Chicago's METRO Achievement Center, a corporate work of Opus Dei that provides supplementary education to underprivileged girls in the inner city of Chicago, tutors a young girl in mathematics.

Inner-city Chicago boys participate in the athletic portion of Midtown Center's Summer Achievement Program, a summer program for boys run by Opus Dei.

privilege on the members within the organization. With regard to the purpose of joining the Prelature, all are radically equal, with the same vocation and the same means of formation."

Indeed, the higher quota of intellectuals is not a chance statistic, and seems to derive from the particular attention paid to them. To refer to the official words of the Postulation we cited previously, "The end for which the Lord has set it moving is that people of all social categories, *beginning* with the intellectuals and then reaching everyone..." (italics mine).

The Way (No. 978) is to the point. Citing the words of Jesus to the disciples, "Come, follow me, and I will make you fishers of men," Escrivá comments, "Not without reason does our Lord use these words: men—like fish—have to be caught by the head."

It is a banal observation, today more than ever, that society arrives at the majority of its ideas and modes of behavior by way of the intellectuals. As Cardinal Paul Poupard, president of the Pontifical Council for Culture, wrote: "Blessed Escrivá has always dedicated the utmost attention to those who work with ideas and transmit them, because in our century as in no other the problem of problems for Christianity is the relationship between the Gospel and culture, and that means the evangelization of the intelligentsia."

Besides this strategy, which is important, there is probably a practical reality tied to the history of Opus Dei. It began with a group of university students that gathered around the young vibrant priest. The first "apostolic works" were thus an academy and a student residence in Madrid, especially for students of architecture and law. And since "like evangelizes like," this Christian message, the message of Opus Dei, made it a priority to penetrate the intellectual milieu before spreading to other environments. In this, too, the "dark tale" is discredited: it is professors, men of culture who pervade the Work, not rich professionals and financiers, as so often reported.

In Rome, for example, Opus Dei residences for university students, the larger portion of whom are of modest origins, as in Pamplona, exist alongside boarding schools for aspiring artisans and hand-workers; and the Centers are in the middle-class quarters as well as the richer suburbs. To take one other example among many, the Instituto Rural Valle Grande in Peru is a large South American project that helps the poorest peasants, and for the most part it is run by peasants who, like so many other *campesinos,* are members of the Work.

"Remember that of one hundred souls, we must be interested in one hundred: the soul of the Andes Indian as much as the financier of Wall Street; the soul of the villager as well as the soul of the Nobel prize winner in astrophysics." This teaching of the founder seems to me to be among the most dynamic in the Prelature. Unfortunately, many Christians today confuse "economic" poverty with "evangelical" poverty.

> *"Remember that of one hundred souls, we must be interested in one hundred."*
> *—Escrivá*

In the true Christian view, poor people are not in any more need of spiritual assistance than rich people—what matters is not income but the attachment of the heart. As Peter Berglar writes, "To treat only the 'poor' with charity is a deformation of the Christian spirit, seeing that the 'rich' (as we know from the Gospel) have a particular need of the grace of God to be saved. And they have a special need for the charity of their neighbors."

And so here, too, a perspective all too human—that sees two opposites in everything, the "powerful" and the "underling"—has besmirched the religious vision, which judges everything in terms of grace and sin, of charity and egotism, of detachment and greed. In Oscar Cullmann's words: "The Gospel does not call the poor to revolt, but the rich to responsibility. By reminding everyone, whatever their social position, that everyone has a need for repentance and pardon, the 'revolution' of Jesus is not a superficial one like those of modern ideologues: it goes to the depths, teaching that there is no improvement in society if everyone, no matter whether rich or poor, does not improve himself first."

What Escrivá said is to the point here: "On the Cross, Jesus didn't stretch out only the right or only the left arm, he stretched out both."

CHAPTER ELEVEN

VOCATIONS WITH A CONTRACT

UP TO THIS POINT, we have tried to understand *who* joins the Work and *why*. What remains to be seen is *how* this takes place, and how you stay once you join. Here, it seems to me, is where the "agency" image is particularly relevant.

Particularly, because one does not join the Prelature by taking vows or through other sacred formulas, but rather by a layman's contract. It is a truly contractual agreement, undertaken in the presence of two witnesses in any location, not in a church, and "without any solemnity or officialism, preserving the private character" of the agreement between Opus Dei and the person, who freely asks to belong.

In the words of Le Tourreau, who well understands this: "In order to place in better relief the secular character of the incorporation, the Congregation for Bishops (to which, note well, the

Work pertains, and not the Congregation for Religious) under-
scores the fact that it does not take place by virtue of a vow. The
bond of the members of Opus Dei is radically different from that
of the religious and from those who are consecrated with the vows
of poverty, chastity, and obedience. The consequences of this are
that the condition and the personal status of the members are
changed very little by belonging to the Prelature: the total
absence of a 'sacred bond' makes it possible for each member to
remain a common faithful lay person of the diocese."

It is really quite simple, if disconcerting. In practice, something like the following takes place: on the one side is the
Prelature which undertakes by contract to furnish a constant doctrinal, spiritual, ascetic, and apostolic formation, and makes available the specific pastoral care—a carefully personalized care—of
its priests. As one document has it, "The institution undertakes
that none of its members be without the spiritual assistance and
formation necessary for sanctification in the midst of the world,
putting into action a kind of permanent training in the interior
life and in the apostolate."

On the other side is the individual lay person who has decided,
impelled by a vocation—they put much emphasis on this—to
make use of the services of this spiritual agency. It is important to
note that the member is both consumer and partner, giving and
receiving something solely on the religious plane, which is the
only matter in question. The temporal surroundings are completely and explicitly excluded from the contract.

The interested baptized person "declares" (as the official terms
state) that "in full use of his liberty, he has the firm intention of dedicating himself, with all his powers, to the pursuit of sanctity and the
exercise of the apostolate, according to the spirit and the practices of
Opus Dei. He binds himself from this moment (until a renewal the
next year, or for a lifetime, but not before five successive annual
renewals, and being at least twenty-three years old) to remain under

the jurisdiction of the Prelature in everything that regards his ascetic, formational, and apostolic commitments, as directed toward the achievement of the spiritual aims of the Prelature."

For the rest, he continues to have the same duties and rights, with respect to his diocesan bishop and the Church in general, as any other Catholic, which in effect he continues to be. He also continues, as any citizen, to respect the civil and penal laws of his country, since belonging to the Work concerns the sphere of religious liberty with obligations that are purely religious in nature. This, remember, is precisely what the Italian minister of the interior discovered after his investigation.

Later on, we will treat in more detail the topic of reciprocal rights and obligations, as a commitment which each party to the contract freely assumes. For the present, we will seek to understand this network of contracts between the Prelature and tens of thousands of men and women of about ninety different nationalities.

The contract preserves the lay character of the organization and keeps the Work from becoming an order or a congregation, and its members from becoming, like religious, bound by orders or sacred promises. To quote Escrivá again, writing in 1941, "We are interested in all the virtues. We are not interested in vows, even if, in respect to theology, they are worthy of all respect; and we do have great respect for them when we encounter them in others. But they are not for us."

If the lay nature is emphasized and secured by a contractual bond, if Opus Dei is not an order, not a congregation, no longer a secular institute, as it had to be absent any better canonical arrangement until six years after the death of the founder, no more is it an economic society, a cultural foundation, a club, syndicate, or league. From the very beginning, the Work has understood that it is a family.

The intention, as expressed by the Prelature, is that Opus Dei resemble the same family dynamism that governs everything within Christianity, which has the Our Father, as taught by Jesus

Himself, as its fundamental prayer, and which consequently invites everyone to be considered brothers and sisters. This is a faith which calls its visible head, who is believed to be the Vicar on earth of Christ in Heaven, not president or general, but the Holy Father, *Papa,* Pope. A faith which, in the last General Council, defined the Church as the "House of God, where His family dwells."

And thus it seems entirely fitting that on the marble slab over the tomb where Escrivá was buried are carved the words *El Padre.* Moreover, according to the statutes solemnly approved by the Holy See, this family title has become an official title. The precise formulation says: "This person, [i.e., the prelate of Opus Dei] must be a teacher and a father to all the faithful of the Prelature, who loves everyone with the heart of Jesus Christ, who takes care of all, who teaches all, who gives himself and sacrifices himself gladly for the benefit of all, in an effusion of *caritas.*"

Monsignor Escrivá affirmed, then, **the equality of all members.**

Do not forget, however, that unlike convents and monasteries, the overwhelming majority of Opus Dei members are fathers and mothers of families. And thus it is not difficult to require that everyone in the Work live a "family spirit." This explains another peculiarity: Opus Dei is a solid block, with no internal differentiations that are not contingent or organizational in nature and more dependent on concrete personal situations than on spirituality.

As Le Tourneau puts it: "Monsignor Escrivá has always been preoccupied with emphasizing the fact that the members of the work all have *the same vocation* to sanctity and apostolate regarding the exercise of their professional work; and that, despite all this, *there are no classes of members,* in the sense that some are more important than others, and that some receive a different or more demanding 'vocation.' He affirms, then, the *equality of all members,* encompassing priests and lay

people, men and women, young and old, celibate, married, and widowed, of every race, profession, and cultural level. The calling for all
members is *complete* and *final*. The oneness of the vocation is mani-
fested in the fact that all the faithful of the Prelature have the same
ascetic, apostolic, and formational commitments."

But how? Are the priests on a par with the laity? In substance,
and in simple terms, we can say the following: one of the basics of
Catholic theology is that every member of the faith, by baptism,
participates in the priesthood of Christ and thus belongs to a
"priestly people." There is, then, a "common priesthood" on the
one hand, because it is held in common by everyone who has been
baptized, and on the other, a "hierarchical" or "ministerial" priesthood, an office of responsibility that serves the faithful. This latter is reserved for those who have been called and who receive the
sacrament of ordination from the Church.

According to the authentic Catholic position, the priesthood of
all the baptized and the ordained priesthood differ not only *in
degree* but also *in essence.* However, in a correct Catholic perspective, lay persons and priests are not so distant from one another;
there is a family relationship between them, they are not separated
by an abyss.

Ever since 1928, inspired by his vision, Escrivá pounded away
to overcome the concept which has become encrusted over the
centuries of a church divided into superior and inferior classes,
with the ordained or consecrated seen as the only members in full
standing. He fought to readdress the laity. And since equal rights
implies equal responsibilities, all the faithful must take the whole
Gospel seriously. Therefore every baptized person is obliged to
become a saint and consequently an apostle. All of them together
are the Church, that is, true to the etymology of the word, the
community of those called together (Greek *ekklesia*) by Christ.

This explains Escrivá's insistence that in Opus Dei the vocation
is the same for all—"the same *sopera,* the same bowl of soup, from

which everyone draws according to need and personal situation," to use a favorite expression.

This message is authentic and rooted in the tradition of Catholic theology. Yet it was contested by authoritative men in the Church, even labeled heresy, and charges were brought against the Spanish priest to the Holy Office, as it was then called.

Escrivá refused to engage in polemics and continued along his path, saying only that "persecution by the good is the worst." Some members (certainly not all) of a religious order pressed these verbal and written attacks. There were some who did not rest with that but felt themselves obliged to visit the homes of the young people who had gathered around Escrivá, terrorizing their parents by assuring them that their children were in danger of damnation because they were following a heretic who was teaching that all were called to Christian perfection, not only those who were "consecrated." It took the Second Vatican Council to declare solemnly that Opus Dei was licit and proper. This recognition was not so much a new Catholic view as a recovery of the genuine Catholic perspective.

Among the five pontiffs and the many bishops, archbishops, and cardinals who have recognized it, I have chosen the statement of Cardinal Franz König, archbishop of Vienna. In 1975, a few months after the death of Escrivá, His Eminence wrote, "The magnetic force of Opus Dei probably comes from its profound lay spirituality. At the very beginning, in 1928, Monsignor Escrivá anticipated the return to the Patrimony of the Church brought by the Second Vatican Council." He goes on, "For those who have followed him, Escrivá has recalled with much clarity what the position of the Christian is in the midst of the world. This is opposed to all false spiritualism, which amounts to a negation of the central truth of Christianity: faith in the Incarnation."

Why do I quote König? Because König is considered one of the leaders, both during and after the Council, of the so-called "progressive" current.

Nor does it stop there. König returned to the theme, prophesying a place in the future Church for the message of Escrivá that we too, in our own small way, have seen in this study. The archbishop of Vienna said, "The profound humanity of the founder of Opus Dei reflected the shape of our epoch. But his charisma, by which he was chosen to realize a work of God, projected that work into the future. He was able to anticipate the great themes of the Church's pastoral action in the dawn of the third millennium of her history."

There is also Carlo Maria Martini, the archbishop of Milan, often acclaimed as the "up-to-date and human face of the Church." What does he say? "The spiritual fecundity of Monsignor Escrivá has something of the incredible in it.... Someone who writes and speaks as he does manifests to himself and others a sincere, genuine sanctity."

Pope Paul VI, the Pope who initiated a series of postconciliar reforms, also praised the Work: "It emerges, in these years, as a living expression of the perennial youth of the Church, fully open to the exigencies of a modern apostolate."

An interesting accolade involves one "Romero, Oscar Arnulfo (1917–1980), religious leader of El Salvador," as found in *Garzantina,* a small Italian encyclopedia. The entry which follows reads: "Archbishop of San Salvador, and symbol of progressive forces; assassinated by right-wing terrorists." In his biography, Jesus Delgado writes: "Monsignor Romero had become acquainted, in Europe, in 1955, with Father Josémaría Escrivá de Balaguer, the founder of Opus Dei, and a friendship was immediately established, because he admired his utmost rectitude and great faith; Escrivá always had self-mastery, even at the most exhilarating moments, and Father Romero found in him an equilibrium between a demanding personal sanctity and total openness toward others. This latter was the virtue that Romero felt he lacked the most, and for that reason the personality of Escrivá was instantly attractive to him. But Romero's interest in Opus Dei had another root as well. The organization had as one of its first priorities to assist the diocesan clergy in maintaining an intense spirituality, a spirit of dedication and faithfulness to the Church, even in the whirlwind of parish duties. This was an ideal that matched up perfectly with Romero's. And thus it was only logical that he was led to cultivate friendship with the members of Opus Dei, even if, in the strict sense, he never joined this organization."

A year before he was assassinated for preaching the social demands of the Gospel, Monsignor Romero made a note in his private journal dated September 6, 1979: "I had breakfast with the *Opus Dei padres*. They told me of their work among professionals, students, workers, and service personnel. It is a quiet work, of deep spirituality.... The sanctity of the layman in his profession is a mine of riches for the whole Church."

> *Monsignor Romero, a year before his death, noted in his journal: "I had breakfast with the* Opus Dei *padres. They told me of their work.... It is a quiet work, of deep spirituality...."*

On July 12, 1975, a few days after the death of Escrivá, the archbishop of San Salvador wrote to the Pope to ask him, "in the name of the greater glory of God and the welfare of souls," to open promptly the cause for Escrivá's beatification and canonization. It is a letter of extraordinary passion in which Archbishop Romero discloses to Paul VI his "profound gratitude to the priests of Opus Dei, to whom I have confided, with much fruitfulness and satisfaction, the spiritual direction of my own life and that of my priests." Among other things he states, "Persons of all classes encounter in Opus Dei a secure orientation for living as sons of God in the midst of family and social duties: this is due without any doubt to the life and teaching of its founder.... Monsignor Escrivá (whom I knew personally) could enter into a continuous dialogue with the Lord, with great humanity: it became immediately clear that he was a man of God, his behavior was full of delicacy, affection, and good humor.... I have known the Work for many years here in Salvador, and I can testify to the supernatural sense that animated it and its faithfulness to the Magisterium...."

Another man of the Church, Cardinal Ugo Poletti, in careful and judicious language used in the official decree of the introduction to the cause of beatification, affirmed that the founder of Opus Dei "has been recognized as a precursor of the Council"—not only for his reevaluation of the laity, not only for his insistence that all Christians are called to sanctity in their ordinary life of labor, but also for his rediscovery of matrimony and family life as a true and proper vocation, on a par with the vocations to celibacy and virginity. *The Way,* No. 27, says: "Do you laugh because I tell you that you have a 'vocation to marriage'? Well, you have just that, a *vocation.*"

The citations could go on and on.

On the whole, Opus Dei strengthened the role and dignity of women in the Church.

After the Second Vatican Council, all this seems self-evident—*after* the Council. On the whole, it appears that in anticipating the Council, the Work did not only overcome a clerical vision of the Church and reevaluate the priesthood of all the faithful. It also strengthened the role and dignity of women in the Church by insisting that the common priesthood conferred by baptism pertained to both sexes—it is not "more" for males, or "less" for females. Here, too, we can spot a "political" point of view, adapted from what is really a theological viewpoint, which could be called progressive.

Why, then, the aggression of the so-called conciliar paladins against an institution which in historical fact appears to have been one of the major anticipators of the conciliar spirit?

There are many reasons, some already mentioned. In substance: Escrivá and his Work looked with favor on Vatican II, which confirmed them in their vocation; Monsignor del Portillo,

Escrivá's right-hand man, participated actively in the work of important committees. But they were opposed to the postconciliar excesses, or distortions—to what has been called the Imaginary Council. That is to say, they remained faithful to the documents, letters, and intentions of the assembly of bishops, considering Vatican II within the continuity of the two thousand-year Tradition of the Church. It was a deepening, a bringing up-to-date, but without any rejection of what was immutable in the Faith. It was not a break with tradition, a whole new start, a Copernican revolution.

Thus Opus Dei has refused to speak of a pre- or postconciliar Church, as if they were two diverse and irreconcilable things. Such a refusal has been recommended by Cardinal Ratzinger, among others. From this stems the Work's opposition to any form of objection or dissent from the hierarchy's authority, to any kind of "in *my* view" approach to matters of faith and morality, to theological adventurism, and to certain pastoral and liturgical experiments.

Many have not forgiven Opus Dei for its opposition, or fealty to the Church. As one biographer writes: "Monsignor Escrivá suffered grievously by the doctrinal confusion that some people spread in the Church, deforming the teaching of Vatican II." His suffering, then, was not about what the *Council said,* but about what *people said* the Council said, thus "deforming" both its spirit and its letter.

CHAPTER TWELVE

BUT THEY REALLY
ARE LAY PEOPLE

WHAT SOMEONE ONCE SAID rings true: "Before the Council, the Work was accused of 'heresy' because it taught what the Council had to rediscover. After the Council, there were new accusations: this time, for the heresy of obeying the Pope and teaching the faith and morals of the Church."

It is an objective fact that the status of "Personal Prelature"—recognized for the first time in the history of the Church with regard to Opus Dei—is an immediate fruit of Vatican II. Without the Council, the Work would not have found its berth.

There are other proofs of harmony between Opus Dei and the Council, such as the optimism about the world and man—one of Escrivá's celebrated homilies is called "Passionately Loving the World"—but tempered by a realistic view about the fragility of people constantly exposed to sin. Unlike almost everything else in the Church, Opus Dei did not have to undergo an *aggiornamento,* since the Work was confirmed in what it was almost uniquely claiming.

Don Escrivá, with tranquil humility, made clear what any observer would have had to admit who knew the dynamism of the Church or of his organization. "Opus Dei will never need to be adapted to the world, because its members are of the world; it will not be constrained to 'catch up to' human progress for the simple fact that its members, just like other people, are the ones who are building the future with their daily work."

It is also true that in the leaden years following the Council, marked as they were with an identity crisis and perhaps a crisis of faith as well, with the consequent loss of numbers of both practicing Catholics and seminary students, Opus Dei went in precisely the opposite direction—it grew year after year, in its discrete but irresistible way.

"Opus Dei will never need to be adapted to the world, because its members are of the world."—Escrivá

To make a crude comparison of numbers, the Jesuits, the most populous Catholic men's order, had 35,919 members in 1966 and by 1990 had shrunk to 23,778, with a rather high median age. The Franciscan Friars Minors fell from 25,272 to 18,738. As for the women, their foremost institute, the Daughters of Charity of St. Vincent, fell in the same period, from 45,048 to 28,999. And it was the same for almost all the other religious families. Many had to incorporate with others to keep from disappearing altogether.

But for Opus Dei, in the same years, there was a continuous *growth,* reaching the present roughly 80,000 members, all of whom are united because they are dedicated to the same vocation—a Work where there are no vows, only contracts, and in which "there are no diverse categories of members"—because all the vocations are always complete and full vocations.

But what about organization? If there is no recourse to diverse categories of members, or different classes, what do the names "numeraries," "supernumeraries," and "associates" mean? And what do the priests do?

As we have seen, the terms—which have unfortunately contributed to the "dark tale"—have a lay meaning which derive from the Spanish tradition. They simply indicate diverse personal situations, and they imply that the same vocation is lived in diverse ways. What really counts—the spiritual commitments undertaken in the service of one unique vocation—holds for everyone.

In order to understand these diverse situations, it would seem appropriate to begin not with the priests, nor even with the other celibates, the numeraries and associates, but rather with the supernumeraries.

The name is deceptive because it seems to speak of something added, incomplete, indefinite. But an official source states that "the overwhelming majority of members are supernumeraries, and this is the normal state of the Work, seeing that most persons, faithful to their Christian vocation, find their way via the path of matrimony rather than celibacy." The men and women supernumeraries represent 70 percent of the members of Opus Dei.

The same source continues: "The supernumeraries are faithful lay persons (single, married, or widowed) who have been called to a complete divine vocation—the same as the numeraries and associates—and who live this vocation according to the possibilities permitted by their family obligations." Therefore it is clear that "the ordinary vocation of the supernumerary puts in first place the reality that matrimony and family life are a real path of sanctification."

But why do the brothers, priests, and nuns (and the numeraries and associates in Opus Dei) not marry? The answer, one of the most complex knots to untie, is this: "Although, according to theological principles, the 'one who is celibate for the kingdom of heaven' (and this means being celibate is to be more at the disposal of God and men) is superior to [someone in] the matrimonial state, this does not mean that renouncing marriage in itself guarantees someone a higher level of sanctity. In every human situation, sanctity (the goal to which all ought to strive) depends uniquely on one's faithfulness to God." In any event, one can be sure that "in Opus Dei, celibate and married are not seen as opposed states, but rather as intertwined and both oriented toward everyone's objective: sanctification in professional life." For priests, this is their "profession of priesthood."

The supernumeraries, then, represent the "normal," the most frequent vocation in statistical terms, and in them is seen most clearly the purpose of Opus Dei—to Christianize the world from the inside through people of the world who are not worldly. The numeraries represent the "skeleton" of the internal structure. They form at present a little less than 20 percent of the total number of members.

We again refer to the official description: "Numeraries are those who have received a vocation from God to live a celibate apostolate and to remain totally at the disposal of the tasks required by the Prelature: the duties are those of direction and formation of the other members of the Work." And further: "They live, usually, in the Centers of the Prelature, but are able to live elsewhere if necessary—for example, if it is required by the conditions of their professional work."

We should not forget that the numeraries—like any other member, that is, like the supernumeraries—have a professional occupation, or normal, civilian work, which they practice. The duties of formation and direction, therefore (except for special cases, when they are temporarily called to internal governmental duties), are carried out during the time they are free from their professional responsibilities: when, that is, another man or woman would be occupied with family duties. And more often than not, that is what Opus Dei is for them.

The insistence on the unity of the vocation extends, obviously, to both sexes. People are called, whether male or female, to be sanctified wherever they are, and by means of their work. In this way, with the obvious exception of the priesthood, there is a masculine and feminine version of each "figure" (numerary, supernumerary, associate), with equal rights and responsibilities, and with an equal variety of personal situations: single, married, widowed, educated, uneducated, poor, rich.

Of significance too is the statement: "The presence of women in Opus Dei not only means that the spirituality and the mission of the Prelature are concerned with everyone, but also that their presence is required for the family spirit to reign effectively (a family with spiritual bonds), and it shows that the Church is truly the *family of God*." These almost forty thousand women do what other women do, in whatever culture or country they are. Quite a few of the women are professionals, executives, employees, managers, business owners, and so forth.

> *In Opus Dei, people are called, whether male or female, to be sanctified wherever they are, and by means of their work.*

Some of the female numeraries are also the housekeepers ("administration") of the men's Centers, and often coordinate this work with other women, who may or may not be in the Work. This work is not done for free or on a voluntary basis, but as a professional job, something to sanctify and to be sanctified in. Although working on the inside, they are paid regular wages and receive other benefits.

And this "domestic" work is really work—in fact, it is one of the most precious and dignified kinds of labor. In the words of the founder: "There will always be many women whose principal occupation will be the care of their own hearth. I tell you that this is a grand occupation which is worth all the effort. By means of this profession—and that's what it is, a true and noble one—a woman has a positive influence not only in the family, but among a whole crowd of friends and acquaintances, among the people with whom in one way or another she comes in contact, fulfilling in this way a task that is more extensive than many other professions."

Escrivá added: "Work in the home is not opposed to participation in all the other aspects of social life: it includes politics, for example. Even in these fields woman can make a strong contribution, always in a way that specially fits the conditions of being a woman."

The key seems always to lie in the "special," "peculiar" nature of each sex. Thus a radical equality of rights and duties—identical dignity before God and man, but understanding that sexual diversity is part of the divine plan of the Creator, not simply a product of culture, history, or traditions, or anything that can be changed at will.

Thus the refusal to accept the ideology of feminism is a true defense of femininity, and the more it is true to itself the more indispensable it is to the world—to women as well as men, to families as well as professions.

Much controversy has swirled around the role of women in the Work, about the numerary assistants. In this connection, the thoughts of Peter Berglar, the biographer of the founder, are relevant. He offers a perspective which is nothing other than the Catholic view *tout court,* but which, through lack of information, is often rejected because it has been misunderstood.

Listen, then, to the German historian: "In our day, one of the most frequent deformations of the image of the human person, with catastrophic consequences, is the disdain for the spirit of service, the suspicion that favoring such a spirit is a wicked fraud perpetrated by the 'powerful' to humiliate the 'oppressed' who are taken in by the deception. It is believed that to serve is the principal obstacle to one's 'self-realization'.... It is already an evil that men do not want to serve, but it is a disaster when women are also infected by such a refusal.

"Many young women submit themselves to all manner of humiliations by working in an office or in a factory, because they consider it beneath their dignity to work in the kitchen, to organize family activities, and to take care of children (even more so if they are their own children, because they do not receive pay and have to abandon a profession in which, they say, they feel completely 'fulfilled'). Countless women and mothers suffer from a chronic discontentment because consciousness of the dignity of their specific calling has been taken from them, a vocation which goes to the roots of humanity itself, and lasts through all ages. They have exchanged it for a false sense of direction. 'It is better to be unemployed,' a young woman once told me, 'than to clean someone else's shoes or make beds. Nobody can expect me to do things like that.' "

Berglar goes on: "You could always ask things of Don Escrivá. God had asked much of him, and for about fifty years he taught that a *serviam!* ["I shall serve!"] spoken in the love of God and, with attention to God, for the love of human beings, is the very soul of the path toward sanctity, and beyond that, is the indispensable condition for a true and indestructible joy in living. Countless times he attacked the distinction between 'prestigious' and 'modest' work; labor and service gain value according to the love that goes into their doing. Even so, it is clear that work, domestic service in one's own family or in other families, has a superior value; and that such work, when it is lived with a love that is concretized in a thousand particular details to create a warm, cheerful household, is a thing completely positive and natural, especially for a woman."

"Let's not forget," Escrivá said in a 1968 interview with a woman journalist, "that people try to interpret this work as a humiliating thing. But it really isn't.... It happens that the person who provides the service is qualified, professionally prepared.... Every social activity, well done, is precisely this: a very beautiful service—the activities of a homemaker is that, just as much as the work of a teacher or a judge.... For me, the work of a daughter of mine who is a domestic worker has the same importance as that of another daughter who may have an impressive title."

Berglar concludes: "Starting from these principles, [Escrivá] encouraged the feminine branch from the beginning to establish schools of domestic culture, where young women would be trained to carry out the work of the home in a complete and modern way, to learn about the technical means and the most up-to-date economic criteria, in order to accomplish this work with love, to be closer to the heart of God. In every part of the world, many women live their vocation to Opus Dei through this particular form of giving."

But let's return to the question, not of "categories" or even less, of "classes," but rather of the "different personal situations" that are determined by the diverse situations in which the one vocation can be lived.

But before moving on to the priests, let me explain a third category, after supernumeraries and numeraries—associates. This is a kind of intermediate position: in common with the numeraries, they are celibate and share most of the other responsibilities. But they are like the supernumeraries in other respects, namely "associates are those who, for reasons of a personal nature, live in an ordinary manner with their own natural family." They can live with their family, or even by themselves; that is, not like most of the numeraries in the Centers of the Work.

The statute says: "In general, the associates, through contracted responsibilities of a familiar kind, professional or otherwise, have less mobility and use of their time than the numeraries. There is not a large difference between numeraries and associates. The category takes account of the objective life-situations of some persons called to Opus Dei: a way of living the very same vocation differently because of certain permanent circumstances. These circumstances cause the associates to participate to a lesser degree in the responsibilities of government, but they concern themselves fully with the same formational responsibilities as the other members, always in a way compatible with their personal requirements."

In sum, the principle is clear: since *everyone* can be called, *everyone* can and should find a way of living that which they have discovered to be a call from God Himself. Each person has the same vocation, but each person lives that vocation according to his or her personal condition.

According to those on the inside, one of the indications that the Work is still in its adolescence is that the number of associates is still relatively small, comprising only 10 percent of the total. But it is expected that in the future, there will be two to three times as many associates as numeraries.

Above all, everything is done not to give the impression—even, unconsciously—that anyone is "superior" to another, or that anyone is a "second class" member. The vocation of the Peruvian peón is equal to

The vocation of the Peruvian peón is equal to that of the most prestigious priest of Opus Dei, even to the prelate himself.

that of the most prestigious priest of Opus Dei, even to the prelate himself. The aim is the same, the spiritual means of attaining it are the same, the hope is the same. This hope is not only to meet Christ after death, but to hear Him say, as He says in the Gospel, "Well done, you good and faithful servant: you have been faithful in small things, and I will give you authority over large things: take part in the joy of your master" (Mt. 25, 21).

CHAPTER THIRTEEN

PRIESTS, AND *ONLY* PRIESTS

AND NOW TO THE priests of Opus Dei... this unusual clergy, which is forbidden even the taint of clericalism.

The founder taught: "With us, priests must not permit their lay brothers and sisters in the Work to provide them with any services that are not strictly necessary. Each one must have in his heart the same sentiments as Jesus, who said, *The Son of Man did not come to be served, but to serve.* So must it be with us." Escrivá added, "Since the vocation is the same for all, the priest has the responsibility of serving his brothers and sisters, knowing that he is one like the others in our house, precisely because he is just like the others."

This may not be easily understood. Every Catholic bears on his shoulders centuries of clericalism on the one side and anticlericalism on the other: both traps are to be avoided. Escrivá enjoined that "Priests should not take from the laymen nor should laymen take from the priests; we should not have priests who encroach on the temporal competence of laymen, nor laymen who meddle in the spiritual affairs reserved to priests." He often repeated the warning: "The priesthood in Opus Dei is *not* the summit of a career, *not* a reward for the few: it is a calling to serve souls in a manner that is at once both equal to and different from that of the other members."

Such directives are facilitated by the Opus Dei "system of recruiting" clergy. This clergy is not and cannot become an extraneous body or a separate caste within this lay institution because all the priests come from the ranks of the numeraries and associates. One sometimes comes across announcements of the priestly ordination (not uncommonly at the hand of the Pope himself) of dozens of persons of every age who represent the most varied of professions—lawyers, engineers, journalists, physicians, professors, notaries, businessmen, army officers, and so on. These would be forty or fifty priests whom Opus Dei has had ordained (or now ordains, since the prelate is a bishop) to begin to take up their lives as clergy of the Prelature.

In practice, this is what happens: after a certain number of years during which the men have "sanctified their work and were sanctified in it," the Prelature asks these numeraries or associates if they are willing to continue to live the same vocation in Opus Dei, but doing a different kind of work—that of the priest.

The persons who receive this offer can accept or refuse with no judgment attached, either way. If they accept, they completely abandon their lay profession and, as the regulations say, "receive the formation in the Centers that the Prelature has set up for this purpose, in obedience to the norms established by the Holy See." In practice, these are internal seminaries. Up to the last moment, they can decide against ordination and again take up their professional work.

The number of priests is planned; at present it is 2 percent of the total membership of the Prelature (about 1,600 out of about

80,000) and it will probably never exceed 3 percent—only enough to meet the needs of the Prelature, no more, no less. It is a protection against the danger of clericalization, which could burden the institution and jeopardize its uniqueness.

This system of recruitment offers many advantages. The most important are these priests' internal duties of preaching and spiritual direction—apart, obviously, from administration of the sacraments. They know from personal experience the spirit of the Work which forged them, a spirit which they are called to perpetuate along with the laity. Moreover, their practical experience in their various lay professions is essential here, where spirituality is formed in the midst of work.

And since they are called to their priestly ordination at an adult age, with years and years of serious religious commitment, they have already been *proved,* and thus guarantee a particular solidity. The erroneous views of so many in the Church today, which focus primarily on "the modern world" or the "contemporary man," probably derive from their inexperience of such a commitment. That is the source, too, of the abstraction and sterility of many priests' pastoral efforts and of the flood of documents on every subject that issues from the new ecclesiastical bureaucracy.

And there is a further advantage. In the dry formulation of Le Tourneau, "The clergy of the Prelature comes from the Prelature and is formed in its bosom. Opus Dei does not take any priests from the diocese, nor candidates for the priesthood." Almost all the founders of religious orders and congregations, at least in modern times, have come into conflict with the local clergy over the suspicion that the religious institutions are "robbing" the diocesan clergy of their vocations. Many of the serious disputes Don Bosco and his Salesians had with the archbishop of Turin stemmed from this very problem.

But since Opus Dei makes its own priests, it asserts that far from impoverishing the diocese of its priests, in reality it enriches it, putting highly motivated priests at the disposal of the local Church—priests who would not have been ordained had it not been for Opus Dei. They may not otherwise have come to the Church at all, since many of the numeraries and associates who become priests have discovered—or rediscovered—their faith through Opus Dei.

The Opus Dei clergy answers to the prelate in regard to the aims of the Work, but in every prescription of canon law it is subject to the local bishop, from whom they often receive specific pastoral assignments; and they are part of the diocesan presbyterate.

But if the suspicions of stealing vocations from the dioceses are put to rest by the Opus Dei self-support and its own recruitment, other suspicions arise in their place, such as that it wants to establish a kind of "parallel Church" which would become an exclusive sect, or antagonistic to the rest of the *Ecclesia Catholica*. As already explained, the canonical structure of the Prelature seems to obviate this kind of danger.

But it will be of interest to reproduce yet another reply of one of its members: "What could these accusations about a 'parallel Church' mean coming from critics who appear to teach that every Christian, as a free, responsible adult (intolerant of instructions from on high), has the right to invent his own church? We all know that in this post-Conciliar period, everyone acts, governs, teaches, and preaches to his own taste, without regard for disciplinary, canonical, or theological norms in liturgical, dogmatic, or moral matters. Isn't it rather pharisaical that accusations of making a 'parallel Church' arise precisely from these sectors, where every person seems to want the right to construct 'his own' church... a church formed from the teaching and behavior of those who distance themselves from the sole legitimate authority of the Church, namely the Pope and the bishops in communion with him?"

The source continues: "From 1928 until today, Opus Dei has demonstrated nothing other than a total loyalty to the Pope and the Catholic hierarchy. As Monsignor Escrivá said in 1967 in *Time* magazine: 'I have wanted to reside in Rome permanently since 1946, to be not just spiritually but physically present in the shadow of the Vicar of Christ. In this way I have had occasion to know and meet with Pius XII, John XXIII, and Paul VI. In each one of them I have found nothing but the goodness and affection of a father.' The behavior of Escrivá (and the behavior he inculcated in his followers) has been completely coherent. He responded to the pontifical fatherliness (and he always asked everyone to respond) with veneration and filial obedience. Is forming priests and lay persons according to this kind of radically Catholic perspective a desire to create a parallel Church?"

These are lively reactions, especially if compared to the soft style habitually used by the Work, which distances itself from intra-ecclesiastical disputes. The vigor of the response confirms how pervasive such an accusation has become in certain circles, and how insidious it is regarded by Opus Dei members—a particular injustice against the founder who insisted on complete docility to his pastors.

But how can they be priests according to the ideal of the priesthood of Don Escrivá? Coming from the field of labor and occupied with the spiritual formation of workers, will they perhaps be worker-priests, will they conform to the popular picture of the priest in short sleeves, completely taken up with politics, sociological ideas, and the class struggle, who participates in strikes and demonstrations against the oppressors?

The short answer is *no.* The clergy of the Prelature, with their impeccably traditional look, are the polar opposite of the clergyman in a ski sweater of the seventies, crying that he wanted to be like everyone else and thought it alienated nonbelievers to speak of God and of Christ.

Forty-eight years after his ordination—during which he placed himself at the service of people from around the world—and two years before he died, Monsignor Escrivá talked about what a priest ought to be. It is a highly interesting manifesto: a biographer has described it as the *Magna Carta* of the priesthood of today and everyday, not "according to Opus Dei" but "according to the Church," as confirmed by the teaching on this sacrament by Pope John Paul II on every occasion. This significant document will help uncover "the secret of Opus Dei."

"I do not understand," Don Escrivá began in a homily in 1973, "the preoccupation some priests today have for confusing themselves with the rest of the faithful, forgetting or neglecting their specific mission in the Church for which they have been ordained. Such priests think that Christians want to see in a priest a man just like themselves. But they are wrong... the faithful certainly want to admire in the priest the virtues proper to every Christian, which are, for that matter, those of any person: understanding, justice, dedication to work—priestly work, in this case—charity, education, tactfulness. But along with this, they want the priestly character to stand out clearly."

"Some priests think that Christians want to see in a priest a man just like themselves. But they are wrong."—Escrivá

Listen, then, to what people expect from their priests, according to Don Escrivá, who wanted just this kind of priest in his Work: "What people want from their priests is that they pray; that they never stop administering the sacraments; that they be ready to welcome anyone, without putting themselves in charge or taking sides in human factions whatever they are; that they put reverence and honor into the celebration of the Holy Mass; that they sit in the confessional; that they console the sick and the afflicted; that they teach doctrine to children and adults with the Catechism; that they preach the Word of God and not the words of this or that human science—even though they ought to know those sciences thoroughly—because it is not science that saves and leads to eternal life; that they have the gift of counsel and charity toward the needy."

"In brief," he concluded, "it is asked of the priest that he learn not to be an obstacle to the presence of Christ in himself, especially when he performs the sacrifice of the Body and Blood of the Lord and when, in sacramental confession—auricular and secret confession—he forgives sins in the name of God."

This, then, is specifically what a Catholic priest should be and what renders him indispensable and justifies his presence and his role. Everything else can be done better—much better—by the laity. It is not by chance that the experience of the worker-priest, generous though it may have been, is short-lived. The workers do not want priests to be people like themselves, not just any trade-unionist, but someone who speaks of God.

Behind Escrivá's understanding of the priesthood are a theology, an ecclesiology, and a spirituality that cannot help but collide with some conceptions of today. It provided one of the most important objections to Don Escrivá's beatification.

But to return to Don Escrivá. He also lamented the fact that there were "some priests who, instead of speaking about God— Who is the only 'theme' they have the authority to discuss—speak about politics, sociology, anthropology. And since they often know nothing about these things, they often fall into error. Even worse, the Lord is not pleased with them. Our ministry consists in preaching the doctrine of Jesus Christ, administering the sacraments, and in teaching a way of searching for Christ, of finding Christ, of following Christ. Nothing else is in our competence."

According to the statutes, the priests of the Prelature have freedom of opinion in every matter that is just that, a matter of opinion, and even in questions of theology left undefined by the Magisterium. They are able to think as they see fit, or as their conscience tells them, in politics, too, where they exercise the right to vote with complete freedom, on a par with other citizens. But they must keep their opinions to themselves. The prohibition against entering into politics is required by their spirituality: "to be *always instruments of unity* in the Church and among men, and *never instruments of division.*" And politics, as Dante wrote, is "the flowerbed that makes us so savage" (*l'aiola che ci fa tanto feroci*).

Significantly, too, the priests of Opus Dei must have "a *priestly* soul and a *lay* mentality." What Don Escrivá meant by "lay mentality" was, I believe, that his followers, if they were called to ordination, strive to be "priests and only priests," 100 percent priests—and to begin by not interfering with anything that is not spiritual, that does not pertain to the service of God.

From this derives what seems to me to be one of the most surprising characteristics of Opus Dei: the cultivation and the defense of the freedom of its members—surprising because it runs counter to the stereotyped picture of the organization. Le Tourneau affirms that "one of the characteristics of Opus Dei, very frequently recalled by its members and much insisted upon by the founder, is the value placed on liberty."

> *"Love for liberty is intimately bound up with the secular mentality proper to the members of Opus Dei."*

"Love for liberty," he continues, "is intimately bound up with the *secular* mentality proper to the members of Opus Dei. By virtue of this mentality, in all professional, political, social questions, each one acts—in the place that he occupies in the world— according to the dictates of his own rightly formed conscience, and assumes full responsibility for his own actions and decisions, with all the consequences that flow from them. Each person is urged to respect, but also love in a positive and practical manner, a true *pluralism,* the variety in everything that is human. To refer to the declaration of the congregation for Bishops of August 23, 1982: 'As regards choices in professional, social, and political matters, the lay faithful belonging to the Prelature enjoy the same liberty as other Catholics and their fellow citizens, within the limits set by faith and Catholic morality and the discipline of the Church: hence, the Prelature does not take over the professional, social, political, economic, etc., activities of any of its members.'"

Le Tourneau continues: "This deliberate choice of freedom by Opus Dei is not the fruit of human calculation or mere tactics; rather, it is the logical consequence of the consciousness that the members of Opus Dei have of being united only to participate in the unique mission of the Church, the salvation of souls. Without a doubt, the Christian spirit dictates certain general ethical principles with reference to the development of temporal activities: respect and defense of the Magisterium of the Church; nobility and loyalty of conduct; primacy of charity; understanding of and respect for the opinions of others; true love for country, without nationalism; the promotion of justice; readiness to sacrifice oneself to serve the interests of the civil community, etc. And as the basis of these principles, that each member of the Work choose among the diverse solutions and possible options the one he deems most pertinent. As Monsignor Escrivá affirmed: 'With this our blessed liberty, Opus Dei can never be something like a political party in the political life of a country: in the Work there is a place (and there always will be) for all the tendencies the Christian conscience can admit, without there being any possible coercion on the part of the directors.' Only the hierarchy of the Church can dictate norms of conduct in contingent questions for all Christians, if it deems this necessary for the salvation of souls."

To return to the Opus Dei clergy: The numerary or the associate called to the priesthood completely abandons his lay profession, in which he may have attained success and prestige. But he doesn't abandon work: his full-time work becomes the work of the priesthood. This consists, essentially, in "collaborating in the spiritual formation of the members of the Work—both women and men—by means of preaching, spiritual direction, and the administration of the sacraments, especially confession."

In regard to the latter, is someone who belongs to Opus Dei obliged to confess only to a priest who is also a member? The answer is: "The founder always taught that every member is free, as is every Catholic, to confess to any priest in possession of the canonical faculties. A member of Opus Dei will be able to make a legitimate use of this liberty by having recourse to priests who don't belong to the Prelature. Nevertheless, it is easy to understand that this will not occur frequently: if the members of Opus Dei are committed to the pursuit of a concrete aim within the Church, it is reasonable for them to choose the specific means provided for them by the Prelature. It is clear that the priests of the Prelature, by understanding the spirit of the Work and the specific obligations of its members, are able to help them and counsel them about living the sacrament of penance in the most efficacious manner possible, which is also a means of direction."

This is mentioned only because there have been, and continue to be, protests that members of Opus Dei make their confessions to priests of Opus Dei. But common sense would suggest that, analogically, there would be nothing strange if a Frenchman made a confession to a Frenchman, a Barnabite to a Barnabite, or a diocesan priest to another priest of the same diocese.

These accusations confirm the bitterness of the strife that this "new" institution has stirred up, even though its precepts date back to a two thousand-year-old tradition. The suspicions, moreover, deal with actions and usages that are calmly accepted in other religious realities, as for example that Opus Dei members should confess to priests who don't belong to the Prelature in order to avert indoctrination, brainwashing, and exclusivity.

The answer is obvious: "Someone comes to us who is inspired by a vocation that is *freely* accepted. And someone may *freely* leave at any point. However, confession to an Opus Dei priest is part of the spiritual direction offered to members."

But to conclude with the origin, role, and spirituality of the priests. Others must be mentioned who in part overlap the clergy of the Prelature, and they belong to the "Priestly Society of the Holy Cross." The complete and official name in the *Annuario pontificio* is "The Personal Prelature of the Holy Cross and Opus Dei" *(Prelatura personalis Sanctae Crucis et Operis Dei),* known for short as Opus Dei.

Given the theological complexities of this Society and its relations with the Prelature, the universal Church, the dioceses, and so forth, I will simply translate from the Spanish an official explanation that is clear and comprehensive.

"The Priestly Society of the Holy Cross is an association of clergy comprising (1) the priests of Opus Dei, that is, the true and proper clergy of the Prelature, and (2) deacons (those who would be ordained) and priests who, incardinated in a diocese, desire to take part in the Society by responding to a divine vocation which calls them to sanctify their own professional labor, that is, their priestly ministry. To fulfill this purpose, they depend on the Priestly Society of the Holy Cross only in that which pertains to their spiritual assistance (it is limited to the sphere of their personal autonomy): this means that every priest remains completely and exclusively under the jurisdiction of his own bishop."

And it continues: "This society, created by Monsignor Escrivá in 1943, conforms to the spirit of the Second Vatican Council which, in its decree on priests, encourages them continually to improve their priestly formation, and suggests joining some specific organization for this purpose. The Society is an association with a spirit which conduces to unity and nourishes, on the one side, the union of every priest with his own bishop, and on the other side, priestly fraternity. Nevertheless, the members are not the clergy of Opus Dei, but clergy of the bishop to whom they are subject. They are not under the jurisdiction of the directors of Opus Dei. The Priestly Society of the Holy Cross is juridically distinct from the Prelature, but the two entities share a complete unity of spirit concerning the peculiar characteristic of Opus Dei: the struggle for sanctity by way of the sanctification of ordinary work."

To reiterate, this Society responds in essence to one purpose: to see to it that everyone, if they are called, can live the message of Opus Dei. But one can enter Opus Dei only as a lay person; priests are excluded from joining because they are already ordained. Thus the reason for the Society: it allows priests to be formed according to the spirit of the Work, and to live that spirit, while remaining a priest of his own diocese in everything that is not a matter of personal autonomy, such as spiritual formation.

It took a whole treasury of experience and ability to find a formula that would allow a diocesan priest to live the spirituality of the Work, if he is called to it, while safeguarding the rights of the bishop of the region. *Nihil sine episcopo*—"do nothing without the bishop's approval"—is the motto of the association.

This, then, is another aspect of the general plan of Don Escrivá: to offer to all without excluding anyone, a training in sanctity and apostolate, allowing each person to stay where he is, changing as little as possible his life in society or in the Church.

CHAPTER FOURTEEN

THE CILICE, THE ANGELS, AND THE MADONNA

AND NOW A LITTLE spiritual "training."

Remember that you join Opus Dei not through a vow but through a contract "by which the Prelature undertakes to furnish a continuous doctrinal, religious, spiritual, ascetic, and apostolic formation, as the specific pastoral care of its priests." Remember also that this contract, like all contracts, is bilateral: the lay person who signs it has the right to receive the assistance of the Prelature, but also has the responsibility to honor the commitments specified in the ascetic, formational, apostolic concepts.

Let's see what these commitments are, in the concrete.

We begin with the *ascetic.* An authoritative synthesis describes it thus: "The ascetic responsibilities concern the fulfillment of a spiritual 'plan of life.' It is demanding, but adapted to the personal circumstances of each member (everything in the work is personal, nothing is anonymous, standardized, or abstract). It leads someone progressively, as if *up an inclined plane* [these words of Escrivá confirm his intention to construct a kind of agency or service station, while respecting the divine mystery and human freedom, to concretize the content of his vision] to find God in one's professional work and daily occupations."

It is not a minor undertaking and could not be sustained by someone who did not have the vocation. Indeed, someone who only had a human, not a religious, purpose in mind would do better to choose more comfortable paths. Concretely? "This spiritual *plan of life* comprises: an intense sacramental life, hinging on *daily* Mass and communion, *weekly* confession, the habitual practice of mental prayer (up to one hour per day); daily reading of the New Testament and of a spiritual book; *daily* recital of the Rosary; *nightly* examination of conscience; a *monthly* day of recollection and several days of retreat *yearly*; *frequent* spiritual communions, acts of atonement, ejaculatory prayers, etc."

This can more than fully satisfy a vocation, but will weed out the hypocrite or the lukewarm. And there is more: "To this is added the daily exercise of the spirit of sacrifice and penance, *not excluding corporal mortification*, adapted to the age, state of health, and circumstances of each one, according to the particular modes approved by the Church, and avoiding every kind of excess."

Consider carefully: the most beautiful body, if dissected, is nothing but a mass of anatomical parts, without any visible harmony or unity. Just so is the spiritual life, and its "instruments" are the means for helping and sustaining it; and just so all the various items in this "plan of life." If they are taken out of their existential concreteness, they seem like a rather forbidding list of duties.

But in reality, according to those inside this plan of life, this is not so. The climate of naturalness and simplicity, of gratitude for one's vocation and for God, Who is the center of it all, turns what may seem to those on the outside as harsh obligations into something simple and necessary, into the "smiling asceticism" I spoke of earlier.

The formation seeks to attain an ideal: to create men and women who are all of one piece, for whom life and work become prayer.

A brief parenthetical note is needed at this point. The term *"not excluding corporal mortification"* refers to the cilice, which has a high profile in the legend that the Work is the last haven of medieval obscurantists. (I referred to this when speaking of the scandal of the anticult movements.) The legend tells us that this practice, in today's world, is an aberrant, morbid form of masochism, unworthy of an adult or open Christian, that it is the old familiar, somber Spain enrapted in bloody fanaticism.

This famous "instrument of torture" is a band of rough wool worn around the waist or the leg, with knots or dull points of wire that press on the skin without penetrating it. Let us hear from a numerary who has experienced it: "Because many people today have lost the sense of penitence and mortification in the spiritual life, they are astounded, if not scandalized to hear that in Opus Dei, *some* members use the cilice for some of their corporal mortification. *Some,* I say, not the majority, and even these for limited periods. There is no cause to be astonished at their astonishment, because the cross has always been a cause of scandal. But today there are certainly people who expose themselves to great sacrifices, if not corporal suffering (in athletics, diet, and plastic surgery) to preserve or regain a certain external image that others can admire. It is equally true that to obtain a certain physical satisfaction, many other people follow a path to drugs which ends not with pleasure but with pain, and real and true 'mortifications' not only for themselves but for those around them who only want the best for them."

"With all this going on," he continues, "there are yet people who cannot bring themselves to understand the profound meaning of a 'corporal mortification' which does not injure the health and which expresses one's desire to be united to the sacrifice of Christ, to the limited degree possible for a poor human being. It stands to reason that in an age where messages like 'Don't deprive yourself of anything' are circulated, it would be difficult to understand the very rationale of penance and mortification. If 'anything goes,' if nothing is evil that has been decided on in full autonomy of conscience; if, that is, there is no such thing as sin, there would really be no reason to do penance. In this way, 'mortification' becomes unintelligible. And this involves the paradox in the Gospel, that 'in order to live you must die in some way.' Like Christ, the Christian ought to enter the tomb in order, like Christ, to rise again to eternal life. This should especially be noted: one of the most frequently heard cries these days is, 'It's my body and I'll do what I want with it.' It is at least contradictory if this permits license for any kind of bodily behavior whatsoever, even if it is aberrant, but makes Christian penitence a cause for scandal" (Raphael Gomez Perez).

If 'anything goes'; if, that is, there is no such thing as sin, there would really be no reason to do penance.

In any case, neither the cilice nor the other "instruments of mortification" are peculiar to this Work: they are part of the most ancient ascetic tradition of the Church and have been used by the saints.

As Escrivá saw it—in line, here as elsewhere, with the ancient Tradition of the Church—penance and mortification are "the prayer of the body"; the recovery, that is—through this material participation in prayer—of the original unity of man, who is not only spirit, soul, or heart. Even those "ascetic exercises" (always discrete, practiced without burdening others, without letting them be seen) are a means of exercising the will in a world that is ever more unwilling, indifferent, and arbitrary. And these exercises can, and must be, not only active, but passive as well—not so much to seek out suffering, but to accept what is given, day after day, in normal life. *The Way* (No. 173) puts it thus: "The appropriate word you left unsaid; the joke you didn't tell; the cheerful smile for those who bother you; the silence when you're unjustly accused; your kind conversation with people you find boring or tactless; the daily effort to overlook one irritating detail or another in those who live with you... this, with perseverance, is indeed solid interior mortification." This is followed by the exhortation: "Don't say: 'That person bothers me.' Think: 'That person sanctifies me.'"

And now on to the *formational* commitments. These "concern the doctrinal and religious formation that the members of Opus Dei receive during their whole lives, in a mode adapted to their possibility and capacity." Here, too, is the personal dimension— each person has his own formation.

Naturally, like a contract, this kind of commitment is bilateral: the commitment of the Prelature "to form," and the commitment of the faithful "to be formed," making use of the means at their disposal.

This type of education "is oriented toward nourishing the spiritual and apostolic life of all the faithful of the Prelature, in order that they cultivate 'the piety of children and the sure doctrine of theologians' and in order that they be persons who are intellectually prepared in all social environments to realize an effective apostolate of evangelization which would find an occasion in the exercise of one's own profession or line of work."

This theological preparation does not form conference-goers or authors of theological treatises, but rather furnishes the means for that private apostolate, the famous friendship and confidence that involves one's closest neighbors, beginning with one's family and co-workers. In sum, this is what is often mistaken for the "occult activity of Opus Dei," precisely because it does not make a public display of itself.

In my examination of this matter, I found a few interesting characteristics.

Above all, there is the awareness—clearly present in Don Escrivá and the Work—that wanting to "convert the world" needs to be joined to personal sanctity (or at least the striving for sanctity), and that this is the first and indispensable presupposition: without it, the recipient of even the best theological formation will end up being "converted *by* the world."

We see here, in fact, one of the reasons for the chaos after the last Council. Poorly prepared Catholics in great numbers were urged to "dialogue" in a "spirit of total openness" and "radical autonomy" rather than act like well-equipped knights, "heralds of the proclamation of the faith in keeping with the signs of the times."

Many Catholics became convinced they had inherited a shameful history, for which they needed to repent and ask forgiveness. They were even persuaded that it was *impossible*, let alone undignified, for the "man of today" to continue to have faith in the dogmatic realities that were "premodern" and must be "reinterpreted," "demythologized," and dissolved into symbols.

These modern men shudder at the very thought of belief in angels. Yet angels are quite dear to Opus Dei. That famous October 2 happened to fall on the feast of the Holy Guardian Angels. Among the few things that Josémaría Escrivá would say about that day was that the mysterious vision took place while he was hearing from afar the ringing bells of the Church of Our Lady of the Angels.

Peter Berglar comments as follows: "Thus the entire Work is found to have been (and ever will be) under the protection of the angels, just as is every human person. As Don Escrivá taught: 'We ought to cultivate our friendship with the Guardian Angels. We all have need of company: company on earth and company in Heaven. Be devoted to the Guardian Angels!' And we know that Opus Dei has been placed under the protection of the Holy Archangels Michael, Gabriel, and Raphael, in its diverse apostolates with youth and adults, with those living a celibate life and those who are married."

Bishop del Portillo recalled how the founder, upon passing through a door, would pause for a moment at the threshold and all but imperceptibly yield the right of way to his guardian angel, whom he counted as a kindly and infallible secretary of spiritual matters. But not only in such matters: "Have confidence in your guardian angel. Treat him as a very dear friend—that's what he is—and he will do a thousand services for you in the ordinary affairs of each day" (*The Way,* No. 562).

In *The Way* as well as in *Furrow* and *The Forge*—the fundamental trilogoy in the spirituality of the Opus Dei—more than thirty points are dedicated to the angels and to the guardian angels in particular: their beneficial function, and the need to honor and venerate them, to make good use of them.

In this point, too, as the prelate Don Alvaro observed, the founder was the first to practice his own counsel of having the "piety of children, and the doctrine of theologians."

The existence and efficacy of angels have always been a teaching of the Catholic Church. And yet, in the *Catechism for Youth (Catechismo de giovani)* published after the Council in 1979 by the Italian episcopal conference, all traces of the angels have disappeared, including the guardian angels, so beloved by the *sensus fidei* of the people.

Born on the day of the Holy Guardian Angels, and to the sound of the bells of Our Lady of the Angels, the Work has held firmly—without polemics, but firmly—to its affirmation of the existence and role of angels.

And now, exactly thirty years after the Council opened in October 1992, the Pope has approved the new *Catechism of the Catholic Church* and the angels have returned in all their majesty: "The existence of incorporeal, spiritual beings, which the Sacred Scripture habitually calls 'angels,' is a truth of faith. The testimony of Scripture is clear, and Tradition is unanimous."

And so, naturally, guardian angels were and are important, not only to Don Escrivá, but to all Catholics. The new (October 1992) *Catechism of the Catholic Church* declares: "From infancy all the way to death, every human creature is surrounded by their [the angels'] protection and intercession." And later an early Church Father, St. Basil of Caesarea, has this to say: "Every faithful has an angel at his side as a shepherd and protector, to guide him in life." It is from this reality, from these angels, that Escrivá exhorted his own followers to ask for intercessions and prayers.

In sum, it is the ultimate confirmation of something a history professor and friend likes to say: "There is an infallible recipe for being up-to-date, and even *avant garde,* not only in the Church but outside of it as well. All you have to do is stay firmly with authentic tradition, not abandon the company of the ancients, and wait. Sooner or later, history will rediscover these things, and you who have been considered an anachronism and a reactionary will be acclaimed as a prophet who could see into the future."

"There is an infallible recipe for being up-to-date, avant garde. All you have to do is stay firmly with authentic tradition."

Opus Dei has maintained a firm defense of another doctrine always held by the Church: Mariology.

The founder of Opus Dei gave prime importance to the Madonna. Among hundreds of other places, consider No. 494 of *The Way:* "Be Mary's and you will be ours." Or an exhortation such as "Count on her in everything and for everything. Do not forget that the Son cannot deny anything to His mother." This position is not limited to devotion or mere sweet sentimentality. Women in general are given high praise, as in No. 982 of *The Way:* "Woman is stronger than man, and more faithful in the hour of trial." This is true Christianity, where humility lives with audacity, gentleness with strength of character and force of will.

There is not the least bit of affectation in the exalted place reserved to Mary, but a conscious reality. To sum it up: without that root of the flesh, which was the womb of a woman in whom the incarnation of God (in the full and proper sense) was achieved, Christianity is reduced to an impalpable and impotent message, a kind of hot air balloon buffeted by the winds, filled with the gasses of a spiritualism, noble in appearance and religious but with none of the materiality of Gospel faith. In his homily, "Passionately Loving the World," Escrivá said, "Authentic Christianity, which professes the resurrection of all flesh, has always quite logically opposed 'disincarnation,' without fear of being judged materialistic. We can, therefore, rightfully speak of a Christian materialism, which is boldly opposed to that materialism that is blind to the spirit."

Mystics and theologians alike have held that "Mary is the enemy of every heresy," and the organic position of the "root of the flesh in the *Credo* secures the fundamental truths of Christology itself.

It was not by chance that, when not only the institutional Church but its very faith seemed to be endangered by the storm of the revolt, Escrivá, who until then had hardly ever left Rome, decided to make some personal significant trips. On the threshold of the seventies, he set out on a series of pilgrimages to the most venerated Marian shrines of Europe and America: Lourdes, Fatima, El Pilar, Einsiedeln, Guadalupe, and others.

And not only that, he hurried the completion of the shrine of Our Lady in remote Torreciudad (to where, as a child of two, he had been carried by his parents in thanksgiving for his sudden healing), in order to construct, in that Marian center, a stronghold of orthodox resistance, a barricade to defend the *Credo* in all its contents.

The founder wanted the Work to have two characteristics etched in its being—to be *Roman* and to be *Marian*. Thus in its work of theological or spiritual formation, the position of the Madonna is that which she has always had in the church, the position she will continue to have, if Catholicism wants to remain as it is—at the center.

CHAPTER FIFTEEN

EACH IN HIS OWN WAY

✝

MARY AND THE ANGEL—and all the other Catholic doctrines of all times—have been reconfirmed by the universal Catechism. And this Opus Dei faithfully hands on to its members. The statutes of the Prelature emphasize that "instruction of the members is presented in a way that is in complete conformity with the Magisterium of the Church."

This is what really counts—what is *de fide*—that is, not "according to *me*," but rather "according to *us*" as in the Creed, proclaimed by the Pope and the College of Bishops and in continuity with Tradition. In short, to cite the statutes of the Work: "Opus Dei does not have its own doctrine and does not establish its own schools of thought in those philosophical, theological, and canonical questions that the Church leaves to free discussion."

Over the centuries, and up until today, many religious orders have given life—legitimately, because within the Church—to spiritual perspectives and emphases, to schools of theological reflection: for example, the Dominican, Franciscan, Jesuit, Redemptorist, Carmelite, Benedictine, Barnabite, and so on.

But not so Opus Dei, whose peculiar element is not to be *original* but to be *normal* even in the doctrine in which its members are formed. It is not the *novelty* that counts (at least in what concerns the institution) but *fidelity* to the Magisterium, which declares definitively and explicitly what must "be believed" *(credendum),* if one wants to be considered a Catholic.

Here, too, is another discovery of the Work's universality: it is not a group of eccentrics, even congenial eccentrics. In fact, it is not a group among other groups but a Catholic agency that proposes a self-improvement program to all baptized persons: to know and thoroughly live, not a particular spirituality, but normal Catholicism.

"Do not forget that in temporal questions there are no dogmas."
—Escrivá

Once again, it is "the strangeness of not being strange," the wish to leave everyone where he or she is, but calling all to live the Gospel radically, without putting on the distinctive dress of this or that theological/spiritual school: *Catholics, pure and simple, without adjectives.*

There is another characteristic of Opus Dei that is not in contrast to but a confirmation of this plan: alongside doctrinal fidelity—and what is "obligatory" for someone to believe in order to be called a Catholic and to be in full communion with the Magisterium, is less than usually thought—is the complete freedom of opinion in matters that have been left by the Church to the autonomous discretion of the faithful.

But there is still more freedom in social, political, and economic questions. We have touched on this in the chapter on priests. To sum it up with Escrivá's own words, "Do not forget that in temporal questions *there are no dogmas.*"

Here we have arrived at one of the nerve centers in our field of inquiry. It is one of the points where the theory and practice of this organization expose, and disprove, the "dark tale" about it. This tale avers that this Mafia-like organization moves in a solid bloc with its faithful knights in defense of reactionary political interests, along the way garnering obscure financial advantages in order to put humanity under the "sacred mantle" of fanatics and hypocrites.

I know this tale, I know it well. And I can attest that the truth is quite different from the myth. The truth is based on countless statements made by the founder; by what his successor has said in the clearest possible way; by statutes and regulations; and by the internal logic that governs the institution.

The Work is united, compact, and homogeneous regarding its own religious and spiritual aims (sanctification *of, in, and through* work with an apostolate of the milieu), and these are its only aims. It is intentionally pluralist, and pluralist to the maximum degree, in everything else: "Loving and respecting the variety of everything human—everywhere, beginning with the Church."

I believe that Escrivá was thinking of this when he defined Opus Dei as "a disorganized organization": well structured, that is, for its religious purposes, but not at all organized "in what is not part of its competence." Thus its members "compose a variegated and multicolored mosaic of free activities, as countless as the possibilities offered by life, character, work, personal history, and culture."

The words repeated constantly by the organization are not merely words: "One of the characteristics of Opus Dei on which its founder especially insisted is cherishing freedom and personal responsibility."

This view is only logical, given the goal of Opus Dei, which was to create and maintain a "lay mentality" and not, therefore, impinge upon areas that, in the world, are left to each person to decide freely.

This freedom and autonomy of choice derive as well from the fact (mentioned earlier) that the vocation required for joining the

Work is perceived, by the person who seeks entrance, as a divine initiative: for ends that are directly and solely religious and spiritual. If the internal reality were found to differ on entering—if, that is, an entrant found himself becoming involved in obscure politico-economic projects for someone's personal gain—how account for the notably few departures from the Work?

Surely tens of thousands of men and women over the whole world could not be persons of ill will and a bit ignoble as well. Or do we have a kind of mass conspiracy here? Does each one, at his own level, high or low, seek his own profit by uniting with the others? No. Escrivá said again and again to anyone interested in joining, "Opus Dei is an apostolic work, it *only* concerns souls. Our principles do not permit us to act like a mutual aid society."

The members agree: "It is unthinkable to want to subject one's membership in the Prelature to personal ends, for professional advantages, or for support or recommendations to climb the social ladder or impose your opinions on other people." And to confirm this assertion they add that the founder urged those members who could in any way help to avoid any kind of favoritism—above all, with regard to other members of the Work. To cite a text by Escrivá: "It is clear that favoritism is contrary not only to the struggle for Christian sanctity—which is the only motive for you being in Opus Dei—but directly and especially opposed to the most elementary moral demands of the Gospel."

Moreover, there are also the clear and repeated exhortations not to practice a "double standard" of morality. Any member of Opus Dei who acts in this way would be stiffly rebuked and exhorted never to do so again.

Nor should the overwhelmingly popular character of the Work in many countries be dismissed lightly. Nor the fact that the overwhelming majority of members are housewives, workers, peasants, employees, and other people of humble station. People in these social circles are hardly able to help their own in worldly affairs.

For example, could the many thousands of housewives and mothers of families be trying to gain prestige and power? I refer to women because, although they are obviously subject to many other temptations, the temptation to have more power, or a prestigious career at any cost, is generally less fervent than that of their male brothers. They are, moreover, more averse to a certain type of hypocrisy, to mixing the sacred and the profane.

Now there are about forty thousand women in Opus Dei all over the world, and from every social origin, from the humblest to the most elevated. Are these a mass of accomplices? Or victims of deception? Remember, the Work "recruits" everybody, including women, but especially those who are not in a position to provide any socio-economic advantages, nor to profit from any fraternal support to that end. It recruits among people who would never have a place in any service club, where people are co-opted only if they belong to a certain social class. It looks for souls to nourish, nothing more.

Listen to the words of Escrivá: "If anybody tried to do it [i.e., use the institution for personal ends], the other members would not permit it and they would compel that person to change his ideas or leave Opus Dei. This is a point on which nobody will ever permit the least deviation, because not only is everyone obliged to defend his own personal freedom, but also the supernatural character of the religious commitment to which each member is dedicated." He concludes, "I therefore believe that freedom and personal responsibility are the best guarantee of the exclusively religious aims of Opus Dei."

For the rest, would-be careerists and speculators would find it much more profitable to take themselves elsewhere. "Whoever knocks on our door, spurred by a vocation," Escrivá wrote, "knows that the Work asks a *lot* (detachment, sacrifice, work without pause in the service of souls) and doesn't offer *anything* on the plane of purely temporal interests."

But, what about the prestigious resumes, the influential positions of some of the members of the Work? When you ask a member of the Prelature this question, you can note a certain fatigue at having to repeat something that has been explained a thousand times and is furthermore self-evident. Any illustrious person, any famous name, is swamped amidst the sea of anonymous faces, the common people, the vast majority.

They also remind you that their success is based on taking seriously the Gospel parable of the talents: to make the utmost use of the gifts received from God. *Doing things extraordinarily well* is the principal instrument of apostolate in work, and gives glory to God.

Consider *The Way,* No. 372: "You stray from your apostolic way if the occasion—or the excuse—of a work of zeal makes you leave the duties of your office unfulfilled. For you will lose your professional prestige, which is exactly your 'bait' as a fisher of men."

Or this point in *Furrow,* No. 781: "Whenever your will weakens in your ordinary work, you must recall these thoughts: 'study, work, is an essential part of my way. If I were discredited professionally as a consequence of my laziness, it would make my work as a Christian useless or impossible. To attract and to help others, I need the influence of my professional reputation, and that is what God wants.' Never doubt that if you abandon your task, you are going away from God's plans and leading others away from them."

The Forge, No. 980, has this to say about work: "You cannot be a shoddy worker!... You have to give a good example to the people around you—relatives, friends, colleagues, neighbors, pupils—in the way you carry out your profession and fulfill the duties your job entails...."

This kind of spiritual impetus brings remarkable results. It is the source of that aura of being first in their class that often surrounds the members. And this is the "bait" they mean to fish with, although some on the outside find this very success a reason for dislike: "If that fellow is succeeding in his career," they think, "and I am not, it's not because he works any harder, but because he's supported by a lobby of priests and brothers in Opus Dei who give him a push." This is the voice of envy, pure and simple. A certain hostility against Opus Dei has its roots in those shadowy zones of the human soul and unconscious, fed by frustrated and resentful persons.

But if someone turns to the Work for spiritual formation, he must not forget that "Not all of us can become rich, wise, famous... yet all of us—yes, *all of us*—are called to be saints." Because, to cite Escrivá again, "All trades have equal value, if they are done well, since their importance depends, in the last analysis, only on the love of God that is put into them by those who exercise them." And he quotes his reply to a high-ranking ecclesiastic who was congratulating him that one of his spiritual children had been named a minister: "What do I care if he is a minister or a janitor? What matters is that he sanctifies his work."

It is a "religious" goal that will not be reached if—as one of the first thoughts of *The Way,* No. 32, warns—the person who seeks the school of Don Escrivá sees in others *el escabel para alcanzar altura* ("a footstool on which to climb higher"). Once again, the end does not justify the means: a career built upon the shoulders of one's neighbor brings perdition, not salvation.

In this respect, it is appropriate to cite the words of Giuseppe Romano, an essayist who is a member of the Work: "The fact that work can and ought to bring us to God does not mean that we have to fall into an ethic of success. It is *service,* not *success,* which moves the action of the Christian in the midst of the world: not an affirmation of *oneself,* but an affirmation of *God.* Work is well done because we cannot offer God a shabby gift: God deserves better. It is also done well, because it renders service to others and while performing one's own role in the world. Finally, it is done well so that all can see the qualities of the believer that derive from being a collaborator with God in the creation and re-creation of the world."

Romano continues: "All of this leads to consequences diametrically opposed to the principles of Calvinist ethics. And this is the most important one: there are no important jobs or unimportant jobs; the nobility of labor does not depend on its exterior aspect. The work that is more important is the work that is done with more love of God. The most humble job can be more influential on the well-being of the world than the most prestigious office. Each member of Opus Dei strives to work as best he can, in a way that is compatible with his gifts, because he loves God and he loves God's world. It is only reasonable that this would make someone 'rise' in his profession, as it is something that happens to many other good workers as well. And this 'rise' will be the instrument of an apostolate, of which Christ will avail himself, to attract other persons through the splendor of attractive and valued human qualities."

But let us return to the related subject—the freedom of a person who belongs to the Work. Le Tourneau writes as follows: "Precisely in virtue of the 'secular' mentality, each member acts in professional, political, and social questions, in the place each occupies in the world, according to the dictates of one's own rightly formed conscience, each one assuming personal responsibility for his own decisions."

Thus in 1982, with the act that erected the Prelature, the Vatican's Congregation for Bishops, to whose authority Opus Dei is now subject, recommended, or "established" the following: "In what concerns their choices in professional, social, and political matters, the faithful who belong to the Work enjoy (within the limits of faith and Catholic morality and discipline of the Church) the same liberty as their Catholic fellow citizens. Hence, the Prelature does not make its own the professional, social, political, economic, or other temporal activities of the members."

And from the information offices of the Prelature: "You cannot attribute to Opus Dei what falls within the sphere of the liberty and the autonomy of the members. They look to us for the means to nourish their religious life. For everything else, they do not what is suggested by the Work, but by their own conscience and profession."

Other texts confirm this: "The freedom of the members of Opus Dei is exercised above all in their professional work: beginning with the choice of profession and the means necessary to develop it under the best possible conditions. They will render an account of the work they do only to the superiors in their workplace, or to the shareholders of their firm, or the official authorities to whom they are responsible. They will never—and the word is *never*—give an account of their work to the directors of the Work."

The same text makes the following precise points: "If the Work has no authority of this kind, it is also clear, on the other hand, that nobody is able to make use of the professional work of the members to obtain privileges and advantages, which would amount to a rejection of the purely spiritual character of the institution."

As to financial matters, some questions continually arise. What do the members do with their money? Can they spend it as they please? Must they turn it all over to the organization? Can they keep some? How much?

According to the official reply: "In the first place, there are no *quotas*. The climate of liberty and trust for the individual conscience should likewise govern the economic solidarity between the adherents and the institution. In the second place, the members are not distinguished according to whether they have more or less money. There are no *members of honor*. Since, as is well known, there is *one and the same* vocation which is lived in different circumstances, these will influence only what the members bring to the Work in a financial sense."

In brief, then, here is a description of what is determined by the norms and customs for "diversity of circumstances," as it is called.

Let's begin with the numeraries, who, as celibates, "have Opus Dei as their own authentic family." In what concerns their professional work—and all, remember, have a profession and a degree of higher learning—everything they earn is for their own support and the activities of the apostolate.

Opus Dei, unlike many religious orders, does not live on alms: each member is supported by his own work, but a common fund is necessary for "apostolic works," all operating on a deficit, and for internal organization, even if this latter is reduced to the minimum; the terror of bureaucratization appears to be quite lively in the Work.

With the professional salaries or wages turned over to the Centers where they live, the men and women numeraries take care of their ordinary daily expenses; for extraordinary expenses—such as new clothing or other personal objects—they ask the directors, who act (according to the founder) "like the parents of a large and poor family." He adds that "the inherited wealth of the numeraries and the associates do not belong to the Work (and *a fortiori* neither does the wealth of the supernumeraries); they retain ownership of their patrimonies and dispose of it as they please."

In sum, the institution "was organized by the founder in such a way that the Work as such, in canon and civil law, owns as little wealth as possible."

One result is that the Prelature owns only the complex of headquarters buildings in the Viale Bruno Buozzi. As for real estate holdings, they are notably inferior to those of the religious orders and congregations. And this is because monks and nuns live in communities that require houses, while the great majority of Opus Dei members continue to live their everyday lives in their own homes.

Even those foundations of apostolic works whose spiritual direction is entrusted to the Work—for example, the ELIS Center in Rome or the university campus at Pamplona or the Midtown/Metro Center in Chicago—belong not to the Work itself, but to organizations of lay members who undertake their construction and management.

This system has generated a swarm of suspicions. There are two different readings of the situation.

The negative view holds that what we have here is a typical system of an illusionary society, of financial Chinese boxes that hide the true owner behind false names.

The positive view is given by the Work. This calls its structure an agency of spiritual formation that develops a sense of freedom and civic responsibility in those who receive the formation. Thus even though they are inspired by the spiritual motives that moved them to Opus Dei and which Opus Dei has nourished, those members behave as ordinary citizens "who exercise their rights just as if they were not members of Opus Dei."

Thus, to quote Le Tourneau, the "works of the Work"—including the money for administration, as well as the various possessions in land and buildings—"are in reality purely private initiatives and for that reason can never be considered, not even remotely, as works officially or unofficially 'Catholic.'" These works "are realized and directed with practices and a mentality that are *lay* in nature: they are founded and managed according to the civil laws of the country where they exist, without benefit of any special privilege. Their directors are the ones who are ultimately responsible to the competent civil authorities."

Therefore, the Work can turn back the repeated accusations which hold that this system of ascribing ownership to a network of lay groups is really a means of evading and escaping legal and financial laws. The truth, they reply, is the exact opposite: by refusing to designate their activities as religious or Catholic, they renounce the many privileges and fiscal benefits that many countries provide. In any case, the statutes oblige "the greatest respect for the laws of civil society." If the formation proposes to create persons ready "to render to God what is God's," they certainly should not forget what follows, namely "to render unto Caesar what is Caesar's." Indeed, all the voices, suspicions, and accusations to the contrary, never, in any country, has the Prelature been shown to have been involved in any economic speculations as such. And they swear it never will happen, for the simple and good reason that it *cannot* happen, in view of the refusal of the Work to take part in anything other than religious and human formation.

To continue with the theme of economic problems, we can pass from the numeraries to the associates. These are persons who "by the circumstances of their vocation, live in the family of their birth, or with some relatives, or by themselves, and they provide, when necessary, for the support of their household. What they have at their own disposal, they give to help the apostolic works promoted by the Work."

Keep in mind as well that "the funds turned over by the numeraries and associates are used for the needs of the members who are ill or in need, and that their families are assisted if their parents are old or sick and do not have sufficient means. This generosity makes sure that nothing essential is lacking to those who had the generosity to accept the vocation of their children."

One document comments, with a little irony, that "this aid is practically never mentioned when people speak about Opus Dei. And this is good for us: we think the goodness is spoiled when it becomes advertised."

Here, if you look behind the words, is a reply to the accusations of stealing young people from their families to become numeraries. This attack is by no means new. It is very old in the history of religious vocations—the tug between a young person's wish to follow a supernatural calling and the desire, which is also reasonable, of the parents to oppose such a choice, even in the case of sons or daughters who are no longer minors, are well balanced, and fully capable of discernment. It happened, to cite a famous example, in the family of Thomas Aquinas. His family imprisoned the future saint and doctor of the Church for a year in the castle of Frosinone. In all such cases, the teaching of Saint Augustine should be followed: *Honorandus est pater, sed obediendum est Deo. Amandus est generator, sed praeponendus est Creator*—"A father must be honored, but God must be obeyed; the begetter must be loved, but the Creator must be preferred."

To continue with economic questions, we now proceed to the supernumeraries, the largest percentage of members.

According to the Opus Dei information office: "They live in their own homes, supported by their own labors. They give voluntary contributions—according to their ability and generosity—to support the apostolic activities of the Work. A 'minimum' quota has never been set. The amount of the contribution made by the supernumerary is always decided by the person concerned, who must take account of the conditions of his life and not prejudice his own family, since this contribution ought to proceed from personal sacrifice and not from someone else's sacrifice, even the closest relatives."

A few points should be noted. Above all—in contrast to religious orders and congregations and even some secular institutions—the organization does not exercise any control over the lives of the members, nor over any aspect of their lives, including economic matters. In this way, they affirm, "the system functions, and functions very well, completely in virtue of a voluntary participation, continually renewed."

This means that a supernumerary who is, say, a business executive with a high income, may give little to his new family, Opus Dei. This rarely happens, but it is never challenged or even discussed. Any intervention by the directors of the Work is out of the question, because everything depends on voluntary giving. And this is as it should be, since everything is based on the vocation and on freedom—on a freely signed contract which can always be rescinded—and on a sense of obligation, responsibility, and per sonal dignity. Whoever wants to make completely free use of the income of his labors can only accept the consequences: nothing or nobody is keeping him in a style of life of his choosing. There is not the least obligation to belong to Opus Dei in order to be a good Christian or to reach eternal salvation.

A discussion of freedom also extends to the topic of chastity. In Opus Dei, the numerary or associate who wants to get married, even at a mature age, will be invited to reflect seriously upon his decision. In the end, he or she will not be prevented from choosing matrimony, a choice which, as we have seen, is esteemed by the Work and encouraged for the majority of its members.

The structure of Opus Dei prevents it from the unhappy situations that beset many religious orders, where brothers and sisters, having made permanent and solemn vows of poverty, chastity, and obedience, can come to consider themselves "prisoners." This has, of course, a canonical aspect; if someone who has made a religious vow wants to be married in the Church, he or she needs a special dispensation directly from Rome.

There is not the least obligation to belong to Opus Dei in order to be a good Christian.

There are also economic and social repercussions, such as the difficulty of finding lay work, and returning to "normal life." Many hidden tragedies have unfolded and are still unfolding amid the tens of thousands of ex-priests, ex-brothers, and ex-nuns of the post-Conciliar era, and not all of these sprang from problems of conscience; they have also been caused by material questions that only an inhuman and unrealistic spiritualism could ignore.

This type of problem does not exist for those few who undertake to lead celibate lives in Opus Dei. Perhaps this very liberty, this choice that is freely renewed every day to God and to oneself, adds to the efficacy of the institution and forestalls the hidden regret or resignation that might haunt the celibate. For them, a controlled enthusiasm for their commitment to faith, however great the costs may seem to those who do not share their view, seems to be the rule and not the exception.

So much for financial questions. What about *politics?* What can we say about the occult role the Work is supposed to play in politics, namely, the "connections with right-wing governments"?

Le Tourneau has this to say on the subject: "Whoever does not believe in the existence of religious ideals and spiritual values capable of uniting men and women in a common enterprise above ideological divisions and interests, will end up with purely political considerations." And then the confirmation: "The members of Opus Dei belong to about ninety different nations and to all the social strata, mentalities, races, and cultures of the five continents. And they all live in their own family and professional environments."

If this is the situation—and it is—another question would reasonably follow: "How can the institution impose a single political criterion on persons so diverse and so dispersed around the world? How could this be done in a matter so contingent and subject to opinion as politics? How could you demand that a Kenyan conform his behavior to an Australian, or a Guatemalan to that of a Filipino, or a citizen of Singapore to a Luxemborghese?"

This French member of Opus Dei goes on to explain how the relationship (or lack thereof) between Opus Dei and politics is to be understood.

Le Tourneau writes: "Monsignor Escrivá has said repeatedly that, in its intrinsic nature, 'Opus Dei is not connected to any person, any group, any government, any political idea.' In an 'Instruction' addressed to directors, the founder tells them not to speak about politics and to show in their actions that 'In Opus Dei all opinions have a place which respect the rights of the Church.' Adding that 'the best way to guarantee that the directors do not meddle in matters of opinion is the awareness that the members of

Opus Dei have their freedom, so that, if the directors tried to impose a concrete position in temporal matters, the members of Opus Dei who disagree would immediately and rightfully rebel; and I would have the sad duty of praising whoever refused to obey, and of reprimanding with holy indignation those directors who had the presumption to exercise an authority that is not theirs.'"

The author continues: "You would have to know what it took for Monsignor Escrivá to found the Work, to understand the heroism of another declaration of his that reinforces the preceding: 'I have long been writing that, if Opus Dei ever gets involved in politics, even for a second, I would be betrayed, and would have to resign immediately. We must not give the least credit to reports that try to involve us in political or economic or temporal matters, whatever they may be. On the one hand, the means that we employ are always straightforward and exclusively supernatural. On the other hand, the members of Opus Dei, both men and women, enjoy the most complete personal liberty, respected by all, with the logical consequence of personal responsibility. It is not possible that Opus Dei dedicate itself to projects that are not immediately spiritual and apostolic, and these have no relationship with the political life of any country. An Opus Dei involved in politics is a fantasy, has never existed, and never will be able to exist; if such an eventuality came to pass, the Work would immediately be dissolved.'"

And then: "The full pluralism that is really lived in Opus Dei does not cause internal problems. Back in 1930 the founder wrote that this is a 'manifestation of a good spirit, a sign of rectitude in our common action, and a sign of respect for the legitimate freedom of each citizen.' The members take personal responsibility for their opinions and their actions. The spiritual bond with the Prelature does not condition their political preferences in any way. For the members, participation in political life is exactly the same as for their fellow citizens: to exercise their own rights, to fulfill their obligations as citizens and express their own opinions, and to channel them in the various systems of participation that exist in the political community to which they belong. To label any person as a member of Opus Dei because of his political opinions, or, if it is a case of a politician, by his intervention in politics, is meaningless."

In sum, our author concludes: "This attitude of profound respect for the legitimate freedom of the sons of God and of a Catholic awareness that dogmas regard only matters of faith and moral precepts, makes it possible that in Opus Dei there are persons of all political, ideological, and social tendencies compatible with a Christian conscience."

What stands out here is the vexed question of the relationship with the government of Francisco Franco Bahamonde and his regime, which governed Spain from 1938 until his death in 1975.

This question has a high profile within the aggregate of suspicions and accusations made against the Work; let me give you one example: "In Spain, for local circumstances that are connected with past history, the presence of three members of Opus Dei in 'technical' ministries of the Francoist government has made people forget that—at the same time—other members of Opus Dei were working in opposition groups and were opposed and even persecuted with every means at that government's disposal."

Leaving aside the "Spanish question" for now, apart from journalists and general suspicions, no documentation has ever appeared, in any country anywhere in the world, of any role whatsoever played by Opus Dei in political controversies. Men and women who do participate in such activity exercise it as they would any other human means of expression, enjoying the same rights and duties of involvement in public affairs as any citizen in a free democracy. But they participate as single persons, not as members of Opus Dei.

The numerary Gomez Perez throws down a kind of challenge that nobody, it seems, has been able to take up: "In more than sixty years of its history, let someone find a single *pronouncement* of Opus Dei in favor of or against a specific political position."

For the priests of the Prelature, however, active political activity is prohibited, except for voting. And they are expected to keep their opinions to themselves on these matters in order not to influence those who seek assistance in anything not spiritual. They are expected to be signs and witnesses to unity, not to division, insofar as they are priests of the Great Priest, Jesus Christ. A point of *Furrow,* No. 312, is addressed to them (and to the others, but according to their differing responsibilities as laymen): "You should not want to make the world into a convent, because this would be a disorder. But don't convert the Church into some earthly faction either, because that would be tantamount to committing treason."

> *"You should not want to make the world into a convent, because this would be a disorder."*
> —Escrivá

According to the statutes, Opus Dei—from humility but also out of respect for the freedom of its members—abstains from collective actions and even prohibits any participation "in a collective way, in public manifestations of worship, such as processions." The same statutes prohibit "the publication of journals and any other publication with the name of the Work." A journal, of course, cannot help taking a position with regard to the problems of the moment. As far as concerns the matter of faith and morals, Opus Dei has no opinion other than that of the Magisterium; on all other matters, it has no collective opinion, but only the free opinions of the members. Only one bulletin is published by the Prelature (whose title confirms its fidelity to the Church: *Romana*), and it is limited to internal news items, such as its apostolic activities, the names of the directors, statistical data, and so on.

Somehow, a deep distrust or disbelief in this behavior stirs up accusations of secrecy and concealment. The Work does not appear publicly as such, it does not take up a position *coram populo* ("in the presence of the people")... therefore, aha! it must be a *secret society.*

As emphasis, let us examine the norms of the *Code of Particular Law,* that is, the statutes of the Prelature officially approved by the Church. One of the last articles (No. 181.1) reads, "This *Code* is the foundation of the Prelature of Opus Dei. Let its norms be held as holy, inviolate, perpetual; the right to make any changes or introduce new precepts being uniquely reserved to the Holy See."

And so, amidst these norms declared with so much solemnity to be *sanctae, inviolabiles, perpetuae,* stands the provision of No. 88: "In what concerns professional activity, social, political doctrines, etc., each faithful of the Prelature enjoys the same liberties as other Catholic citizens. The authorities of the Prelature, however, must abstain from giving any counsel in matters of this nature. Therefore this full liberty can be diminished only by the norms that apply to all Catholics and are established by the bishop or Bishop's Conference."

In short, and once again: The members of Opus Dei do not receive anything other than spiritual instructions, they do not operate as a herd in political matters, but consider respect for pluralism in matters not of faith one way of obeying a central conviction of the founder.

Here is a passage from a homily by Escrivá: "A man conscious that the world—and not only the Church—is the place where he finds Christ, loves that world. He endeavors to become properly trained, intellectually and professionally. He makes up his own mind with complete freedom about the problems of the environment in which he moves and he takes his own decisions in consequence." He immediately added: "But it would never occur to such a Christian to think or say that he is descending from the temple to the world in order to represent the Church, or that his solutions are the 'Catholic solutions' of these problems. That does not work, my sons! An attitude of this kind would be *clericalism,* 'official Catholicism,' or whatever you want to call it. In any case it means doing violence to the very nature of things."

From this Don Escrivá derives certain precise directives which are a kind of "manifesto" of Opus Dei in regard to its engagement with society and politics: "Above all, you must foster everywhere a genuine lay mentality, which will lead to three conclusions: (1) to be sufficiently honest so as to shoulder one's own personal responsibilities; (2) to be sufficiently *Christian* so as to respect those brothers in the faith who, in matters of opinion, propose solutions different from what each maintains; and (3) to be *catholic* so as not to use our Mother the Church, involving her in human factions."

Note, among other things, how an attitude of tolerance derives from such a perspective, an attitude in sharp contrast with what is commonly thought about this institution, cast in the image of the Grand Inquisitor.

Escrivá had a special reply to make about those who did not believe in the freedom his followers enjoyed: "These are people with a single-party mentality in politics as well as religion. Thus it is difficult for them to believe that others are capable of respecting the freedom of others. They attribute to us the totalitarian and monolithic character of their own groups or parties."

Then, too, Escrivá was attacked by the traditionalist Catholics who would like the faithful to follow them and be guided even in temporal choices. To these Don Escrivá would reply, "Whenever I preach—or rather shout out—my love for personal liberty, I observe in some of the faithful certain signs of disquiet, as if they suspected that the defense of liberty brought danger to the faith. But let such weak-spirited ones be reassured, at least on this...."

To his own, then, he recommended freedom for themselves as well as for others: "Violence, never! I do not understand it—it is not fit for convincing or for winning!" And in *Furrow,* No. 867, "A violent person always stands to lose, even though he may win the first battle." His recipe is this: "Error is fought and defeated by prayer, by the grace of God, by dispassionate argument, by studying and encouraging others to study. And by charity."

On the whole, it seems that the social project of Opus Dei is not having any project, or any doctrine, at least in the way ideologues, utopians, and revolutionaries do. It is not a scheme for a "better world," drawn up on a table. It is the wisdom that there is no way of improving humanity other than improving human beings—one by one, and profoundly. And this is done not by parties, committees, treatises of political propaganda, nor any clerical theories, but by daily and persistent labor, beginning with oneself, in restraining, and—if possible—lessening the traces of original sin in men's hearts.

CHAPTER SI

DARK SHA

norms for avoiding *secretum*
hat "in every region the name
n to everyone, as well as the
verning Council." Also, "At
are furnished not only of the
it also of the directors of the
the same diocese."

mething we already know
mility, Opus Dei is not able
d of publication under the

arise particularly about the
n: Opus Dei provides the
, and the directors of the
ie names of any other mem-
lden," or "suppressed"? Or

omez Perez: "The Prelature
HAVING TRIED TO DISMANTI cy of its members. Thus it
of this institution called Opus Dei, icate the condition of mem-
stood, seems disconcertingly simp t wish it." The same author
to fathom the recurring accusatic to be ignorant of the habi-
it is a "secret society," a "hidden r that depends on voluntary
freemasonry."

Most recently, we have seen ho fessor of anthropology and
allowed to the members—everythin a book further facts and
and morals defined by the Magist ase his judgment.
ple. Opus Dei, they conclude, does ot entitle his explanatory
not come out into the open... there *cusations of Secrecy or* some-
ity, the Prelature does not express *ncillez de las manifestaciónes,*
neither has them nor can the *in Behavior.* Thus "a desire

Now, in the course of researchi ness" or "simplicity." And
other "anomalies"—aspects of the w ld like us to consider.

This is what he says: "A member of Opus Dei—who is someone who performs some kind of labor within society—does not go around shouting to the four winds about his responsibilities to the Prelature. He does not announce he is a member on his business cards nor put it on his *curriculum vitae*. To all intents and purposes, his membership in Opus Dei is a private matter. But at the same time, since he carries out a personal apostolate among his relatives, friends, and acquaintances, his standing as a member of Opus Dei is in fact known by them. Not 'shouted to the four winds,' but known. This characteristic of Opus Dei's spirituality, which has been a constant from the very beginning, has often been misunderstood, so that it gets transformed into a stereotype: the *'Secret of Opus Dei.'* This is combined with another stereotype, the 'conspiracy,' which has victimized, in turn, Jews, Christians, Protestants, Catholics, Communists, anti-Communists, and in general any combination of persons that can be identified as a 'group.' And Opus Dei has been a victim of this syndrome, even though, for some time now, the accusation of being a secret conspiracy, or simply something 'hidden,' has been exposed as fossilized misinformation which lingers by mere inertia."

Gomez Perez continues with a phrase we have already noted but which is worth repeating: "The Prelature of Opus Dei has the obligation to respect the privacy of its members. This means it has no right to communicate the fact of membership if the person in question does not permit it. To confuse this with 'secrecy' is to be unwilling to recognize the standard practice of any organization with voluntary contracts." Recall that in the Work the members are not bound by vows or promises, but by a bilateral contract. In this it differs drastically from traditional religious organizations.

Gomez Perez continues: "In reality, as already explained, the condition of being a member of Opus Dei is known, at least, within the family and professional environment of each person.... There is no desire to be secret, for example, when you respond evasively if someone, without knowing you, asks what bank you use. That is certainly not 'secret' information, since many people already know it."

He goes on: "The difficulties of understanding this aspect of the spirituality of Opus Dei arise from an idea that has taken root, that a spiritual commitment needs to be advertised on the exterior by some kind of 'showy' sign. The religious have always worn special habits, so that their religious profession could be immediately known in its exterior aspect. Now: the condition of the members of the Prelature is not, as I have repeated several times, a 'religious' one. The priests of the Work are secular priests. The laymen in the Work are, above all, what each one of them desires to be or has become: employees, engineers, doctors, students, athletes, singers, professors, secretaries, lawyers, farmers, salesmen, bankers, mechanics, and so on, over the whole gamut of occupations in society. To be in Opus Dei is not a profession, but a spiritual vocation. A member of Opus Dei will speak of it when it is spontaneous and normal for him to do so, among friends and acquaintances."

To be in Opus Dei is not a profession, but a spiritual vocation.

At this point, Gomez Perez speaks of an element cited earlier from articles of the Prelature's statutes: "This *non-spectacular* style, a 'natural' lay style, is connected with something which often appears in the writings of the founder and in the norms that govern the institution: personal and collective *humility.* On the first of these, there is complete unanimity among spiritual authors, who affirm that pride is the worst enemy of sanctity, and not surprisingly is considered the worst of the seven capital sins. But Opus Dei is especially concerned with teaching its members about the importance of the second kind of humility as well. There is no call for seeking the glory of Opus Dei because its glory is to live without human glory. The principal reason behind this attitude is the conviction that glory is owed to God alone—

Deo omnis gloria. This ancient Christian aphorism was frequently repeated by Monsignor Escrivá. It works together with historical experience, which teaches that Christian institutions that want to defy obsolescence should not exalt their *esprit de corps.* The apparent advantages of this in the beginning become transformed, in time, into something dangerous: if the foundational purpose is lost sight of, the actual object of the institution becomes 'being respected,' having an influence, being present, having a 'finger in every *salsa,*' and so on. While this is less dangerous in a political or cultural enterprise, it can be fatal for an institution with spiritual and apostolic ends."

To bring still more force to the argument, I offer the written statement of a director of the Work whom I contacted in preparing this book. He wrote: "The fact that the statutes make no mention of any form of 'publicity' for members who are simply members—lay persons who have no special governing function within the institution—does this not underline the Christian *normality* of being a member of Opus Dei? On the other hand, the stubborn search for 'public information,' or for 'publicized lists' of these simple members—who is asking for this? In fact, if the members of Opus Dei are truly what they say they are, at least two things follow. *First,* that in fact, the people who know them know that they are members of Opus Dei. *Second,* that this does not interfere with their civil, professional, political, etc. actions. They are common people, common Christians, and they desire to be judged as such. Now, since this is the case, what motivation could there be to make public the label 'member of Opus Dei,' to make it known noisily to a limited number of citizens? If the suspicion of an 'incompatibility' between 'obedience to the State' and 'obedience to an institution' on the part of Opus Dei members has been publicly, officially, and authoritatively overcome, the one possible motive that remains is that this is a voluntary, discriminatory persecution. In other words, whoever wants the 'publication' of the names of the members denies that the members of Opus Dei are 'common citizens.' They are either sincerely convinced of this or they pretend to be. In the first case, all they need is to be better informed. In the second case, someone is engaged in actual prevarication for his own purposes. The only imaginable justification for this would be the isolation of the members and their removal from public life in some fashion. It is to 'point a finger' at them and to try to render their actions ineffective—citizens who would like to exercise their legitimate freedom to live the Christian faith in an authentic manner, a faith that is all the more authentic through not having labels, proclamations, and promises."

Here is one final bit of news that I have obtained from a recent interview with the Catholic philosopher Rocco Buttiglione. Responding to questions about the connections which are always coming to light among masonic lodges, organized crime, political movements, and financial enterprises, this philosopher made what appears to me a practically incontestable observation: "When we speak about freemasonry, the question about Opus Dei seems always to rise. Let's say, just by way of hypothesis, that Opus Dei puts much emphasis on being reserved, whether this is justified or mistaken. The comparison, however, is improbable, since the members of this Prelature, even if they don't broadcast the fact that they are members, are proud of their Catholic identity, and they are obliged to manifest it openly. If, continuing to speak hypothetically, we didn't know whether a given person was in Opus Dei, we could still know clearly and with certainty that the person is a convinced and practicing Catholic. Someone who belongs to an anticlerical organization will never be in a position to discover, to his surprise, that his own secretary is a member of Opus Dei. And this creates an insurmountable difference with respect to freemasonry."

To conclude our journey through the "dark shadows," let's move to Spain, from the beginning of its Civil War in 1936 to the death of Franco in 1975. Objectivity requires me to mention three items.

First, and above all: the relationships between some members of Opus Dei and Francoism are considered by Opus Dei as "a particular Spanish case." It is not something central, as is sometimes made out by the critics of the organization. In fact, further confirmation that the vision was supposed to be extended to the whole world, and not limited to a single country and one definite time, can be found in Don Escrivá's immediate plan to move to Rome. He was impeded, of course, first by the Civil War, then by the Second World War.

By 1946, when both wars were over, he took an old steamer from Barcelona to Genoa and soon after reached the city where he would permanently reside, establishing there the seat of a Work that was going to be universal, and which could therefore realize its worldwide mission in this Catholic city. He wanted Opus Dei to be Roman and Marian.

Today, the great majority of members are non-Spanish, even though Castilian continues to be a kind of *lingua franca.*

In reply to the American interviewer of *Time,* during the sixties when Francoism was still in full force, Monsignor Escrivá said, "In very few places have we had fewer facilities than in Spain. I don't like to say so, because I naturally love my country deeply, but it is in Spain that we have had the greatest difficulties in making the Work take root.... The situation in Spain with respect to our corporate apostolates has not been particularly favorable either. The governments of countries where Catholics are a minority have helped the educational and welfare activities founded by Opus Dei members far more generously than the Spanish government.... Today, however, Spain is only one of sixty-five countries where there are persons in Opus Dei. If geographical situation has helped it there, from the beginning it had a universal scope."

Thus we must look at the "case of Franco," but with an awareness that it is not an objectively central fact but a marginal one. Certainly the matter was bound to a precise time and place and is now definitively past.

There is a second consideration, also connected with objectivity.

A source in the institution says, "It should be a mystery for those who speak of a *powerful Opus Dei political lobby* which was supposed to have spread its tentacles over the public life of Spain in the wake of Franco's death. In fact, this lobby did not intervene at all, so that from 1976 to 1982, Spanish politics certainly did not develop as the Work might have wanted, at least in view of the political project that was falsely attributed to them. And beginning with 1982, the mystery gets murkier, for in that year a socialist group took power that was not the least disposed to favor the Church or Catholics in any way, and was even opposed to religious experience as such. The Iberian peninsula suffered a violent, rapid secularization that showed some phenomena of advanced de-Christianization. And where is that lobby now? That Mafia that so many swore was ready to influence every aspect of its native country—from politics to economics to culture?"

It is an interesting question, and deserves an answer.

A third and last consideration: We refer to the words of Peter Berglar: "The members of Opus Dei that had any profile in government during the last years of Franco's rule acted in the exercise of their rights as free persons and citizens of the country. The imitation of Christ, the faithfulness to the Church, and the spirit of the Work did not keep them from serving the Spanish state which, unlike other instances of the past or present, never had the characteristics of an inherently criminal state (and in fact it has never been that). Whoever declares that a Christian can speak only in favor of a democracy of the Anglo-American or Jacobin type, as if only that kind of a system were compatible with Christianity, is adopting an unacceptable, false position."

What this means is that certain voices of scandal who are also Catholics seem to have lost the classical, traditional perspective, still valid today, and have adopted instead prejudices and obsessions, borrowed from contemporary ideologies, which are becoming absolutized. Let's see, briefly, how the matter stands.

Human beings, it is known, can organize themselves according to three fundamental models, which are in practice, of course, modified and combined in various ways: *monarchy, aristocracy, democracy.* The Church has always shown that it does not favor any of these models in the abstract, and does not exclude any of them *a priori.* The actual choice depends on the times, history, and characters of the people in question.

Therefore, if the last few Popes have seemed to prefer the representative parliamentary system, they are also very careful not to make it a dogma, as if it were the only acceptable form of government for a Catholic.

To put it simply, they judged what was the most opportune government for those times and for those countries. For the same reasons, the Church did not regret having had chaplains in the court of the *ancien regime,* or having considered the aristocratic Venice a *Respublica Christiana.*

In those times, in those places, with those histories and those temperaments, the arrangements functioned well. It had to do, above all, with legitimate authorities, to whom the severe precept of the Apostle Paul applies: "Let everyone be subject to the constituted authorities; there is no authority except from God, and these persons would not be authorities if God had not established them as such. Whoever opposes authority, opposes the order established by God. And those who oppose it will bring upon themselves condemnation.... It is necessary to be submissive, not only by the fear of punishment, but also for reason of conscience.... Render to everyone what is due to them, tribute to whom tribute is due, fear to whom fear is due, respect to whom respect is due." (*Romans* 13, 1 ff; 5, 7)

Since the Church cannot take its own road, cannot invent a second revelation according to the tastes and varying requirements of men, but must serve the Word of God, the concrete Catholic behavior toward various governments will be judged according to this passage of Paul and other passages scattered throughout the New Testament. Among which, in the first letter of Peter (2, 17), is the exhortation that in a way synthesizes the Christian praxis: "Honor all, love your brothers, fear God, revere the king."

INDEX